YOUR RESTAURANT SUCKS!

EMBRACE THE SUCK.
UNLEASH YOUR RESTAURANT.
BECOME OUTSTANDING.

DONALD BURNS
THE RESTAURANT COACH™

Introduction by Eva Ballarin, International Speaker, Analyst & Hospitality Lecturer

BY THE SAME AUTHOR
Outstanding Mindset: How to Set Yourself and Your Restaurant Up for Success Each Day! (2019).

Your Restaurant STILL Sucks! - Stop playing small. Get what you want. Become a badass. (2019).

Dedication

To my brothers in the United States Air Force
Pararescue who all live by the Code:

These things I do, that others may live.

My Kempo Karate Instructor, the late Hanshi Terry Lee Bryan
You gave me the best advice I ever received in only five words....

You'll want to quit, don't.

To my Restaurant Coaching Clients:
Love what you do, and you will set the world on fire.

Table of Contents

*"The truth will set you free,
but first it will piss you off."*

Joe Klaas

"Okay, you won't like this: If your restaurant sucks, it's because you suck at running it."

Donald Burns, The Restaurant Coach™

EXPLICIT LANGUAGE AHEAD

AUTHOR'S NOTE:

As you read these words on the following pages, please remember that they are merely words and they lack two of the three critical elements of effective communication: tone and non-verbal body language.

If you have seen me at a workshop, keynote event, or attended one of my workshops, you'll have a greater sense of the positive nature of my tone and the accompanying enthusiastic non-verbals. **Please know that my only intention is to help you reach your true potential.** If the words ahead offend you or piss you off, remember they are only words on paper, and *you* are adding *your* tone to them.

Relax, embrace the suck, take the lessons, and just let that negative shit go.

If you are sensitive to language, you might want to **stop** reading here. The material in this book is written in real-world terms and uses language that occurs in restaurants.

Please note that I don't use profanity to offend anyone. I use strong language to break your thinking patterns and make you uncomfortable. When you get to that place, then (and only then) will you start taking action to make changes.

INTRODUCTION

To Make It, You Need to Be Canalla

Speaking loud and clear is something that not everyone is capable of doing. You have to be an expert, have high standards, and be a little (as they say in Spain), "canalla" (edgy, a rascal) touch to tell often uncomfortable truths, and in a world as complex as the restaurant business, you often hear more of what I call "cheerleaders" who cheer on the initiatives of a chef or owner than those who are critical. Donald is one of those professionals ready to tell anyone a thing or two that they need to hear.

With a direct, vehement, and incisive style, Donald can shake the subject and throws people out of their comfort zone to challenge them out of mediocrity. Donald confronts reality and the need to go beyond doing what has "always been done."

In this book he does not reveal great secrets, or show a magic formula, just commitment to common sense, effort and the desire to leave the average and conformist of your operations and question all aspects that give value to your business. In a business environment as competitive as Horeca (Hotel, Restaurants, and Cafes), in which trends are an overwhelming force that blows up what worked yesterday, techno digitalization is a fabulous lever for change and the human factor is decisive for ultimate success, in Donald's words we find references to not lose compass and work in the right direction to turn a restaurant into a healthy (wealthy) business.

If you are reading this prologue it is because you have just taken the first step, I invite you to devour it and to draw your own conclusions, and above all to enjoy a sincere and direct conversation.

Eva Ballarin

International Speaker, Analyst & Hospitality Lecturer
www.evaballarin.com

Take a Deep Breath and Die

I held onto the wall gasping for air. I was in the middle of doing an exercise called "crossovers." I had 10 seconds to breathe then hold my breath, drop down to the bottom, swim across an Olympic size pool with an empty air tank on my back, try to avoid the instructors providing "harassment", make it to the other wall, go up the side, get 10 seconds to breathe and do it all again.

Why would anyone do this to themselves? Isn't this a book about restaurants?
Stick with me for a moment…

I grew up in the restaurant business. My father was an old school executive chef who was trained by a German chef who would throw knives at his cooks (he would make Gordon Ramsey seem like a nice guy). Training in my father's kitchen was no picnic for any young cook and his son; it was my real-life version of Hell's Kitchen. I'd start out working the prep station, work my way up the brigade system, do something to piss off my father, and be back turning vegetables.

At one point, my father told me that "Cooking is in your blood." I seriously wanted a transfusion. So, I did what many young men did when escaping a dominant parental figure, I joined the United States Air Force (*at the time it seemed a good idea*). It was more like jumping out of the frying pan and into the fire.

A LIFE-CHANGING DECISION

I enlisted with a guaranteed job to be a Russian Linguist. During basic training, a sergeant came into the classroom to show a film about an elite team… Pararescue. These men did combat rescue in extreme conditions. Scuba, tree jumps, HALO, fast roping off the back of a helicopter…. okay, that got my attention. My life had already been about being the best. At 16, I received my first-degree black belt in American Kempo Karate. By 18, I had reached the rank of second-degree black belt (I currently hold the rank of 5th Degree Black Belt in Kempo) and was also taking *Shōrin-ryū* Karate as well as studying Arnis (Filipino stick fighting). Trying out for a Pararescue position was a logical option, and it sounded a lot more exciting than a language school.

Pararescue is the Special Operations Team for the United States Air Force. Each branch of the military has specialized operatives that perform unique missions. The Navy has the SEAL Teams. The Army has The Green Berets. The Marines have Force Recon, and the Air Force has **PJ's** or Pararescuemen. Their sworn duty is to rescue and recovery personnel in combat situations. As a PJ, you're trained in combat survival, parachute skills (you attend both Army Airborne and Halo Schools), Army Combat Diver School (SCUBA), mountain rescue, water rescue, paramedic training, aircrew training, and tactical training.

PJ's are the definition of "Bad Ass Combat Medics."

After you "try out" for a class and get in, the real fun begins. The first 9-weeks is called indoctrination (or Indoc), and it's where most PJ candidates drop out or S.I.E (Self-Initiated Elimination). The majority of guys are good with normal physical demands like timed runs and calisthenics. The timed swims take out a few because some people might be fast as hell on land, however, get them in a pool with fins and a mask on and they find out quickly this is a different world. Then they start to thin the team out by throwing in what is known as "water harassment." It starts simply with a buddy breathing exercise.

Buddy breathing is when you and a partner keep your head under water and pass a snorkel back and forth to share air. Sounds easy right? Not so fast... The instructors start to turn up the heat and will put their hand over the end of the snorkel, just when you are about to get a breath. No air? Now what? The ones that make it just pass the snorkel across to their buddy and wait for another turn. The ones that panic get eliminated. The stakes are too high in a combat rescue situation to panic. Now the physical elements take a turn into the psychological realm.

BACK TO CROSSOVERS

There I was, clinging to the wall, gasping for air. I'd lost track of how many times I had been back and forth. I also lost track of time how long I had been holding onto the wall. It must have been way over the ten seconds because I remember two instructors screaming at me too, "get off the wall!" The louder they screamed, the tighter I held onto the wall. Then (the commandant)

Master Sergeant Clegie Chambers slowly walked over to me. Master Sergeant Chambers was an intimidating man. Tall, burly and sporting a big 80's mustache like Tom Selleck in Magnum PI. He crouched down by me and took off his aviator sunglasses. He calmly said ten words that changed my life forever: **"The easiest thing for a man to do, is quit."** Then he added, "Now, get off my fucking wall." *I took a deep breath and never looked back.*

Almost two years later, I stood on stage with fourteen other men who made it through what is known as "the Pipeline or Superman School," it's one of the longest special operations training courses in the world. It also has one of the highest attrition rates in the entire U.S. special operations community at approximately 80-90% (some classes have only graduated two people). I had become a member of a brotherhood that even after I left the military after four years would have a never-ending impact on my life. Becoming a member of the Special Operations Community (or Spec Ops) has given me an edge in the restaurant industry. The lessons I learned about high-performance teams and becoming relentless in my approach to goals are ingrained into my mindset. You'll never know how far you can go until you push yourself past your comfort zone.

> *What is your limit?*
> *What is your maximum effort?*
> *How far can you take your restaurant?*
> If you are the kind of person I think you are, then you need to find out.
> *That's what this book is all about.*

This book is the real deal. I will share with you how to truly unleash your restaurant by showing you the things that are stopping you from getting the restaurant you know deep inside that it can be.

I am not going to give you a new checklist. Trust me the last damn thing you need is another checklist or software that will sit on your computer (or clipboard) and not be utilized. *I'll leave that to those other restaurant "experts" out there who want to sell you their stuff & systems.*

You see, I'm sure you've tried many systems and restaurant software programs. Maybe you've seen some results. I envision that most likely, you did not get the results you wanted. It's not that the systems are bad; it's just that they are not the **real** solution.

FOCUS ON THE RIGHT 80%

Have you heard of an Italian Economist, Vilfredo Pareto? He discovered a very unusual pattern of input versus output, and it all started in his garden. Eighty percent of the peas were produced by just 20% of the pea pods. It made him wonder if that strange imbalance was just in his garden. His research showed it was not just green beans. He uncovered that 80% of the land in Italy was owned by just 20% of the population. Thus, the Pareto Principle was born. Known also as the 80/20 Rule, it states that roughly 80% of your results come from only 20% of your activities.

When it comes to getting results for your restaurant, I can say with 100% certainty (from working with over 400 restaurants a year) that *20% is systems* and **80% is mindset**!

No bullshit. It's not that system, software, or process that you think of as a silver bullet to fix all the things that are wrong with your restaurant. Those are external tools. Your 80% is the mindset you and your team have. Like Dorothy in the Wizard of Oz, *you have always had the power*, you just never realized it!

That's why those new checklists, new software, and new systems never get the results you want. You're focused on the wrong end of the equation. You're focused on the 20%.

This book was written to get you refocused on the real solutions to create the ideal restaurant you know it can become. We are going to stop looking outside for solutions and shift to that internal element that will finally unleash your inner genius and create your ideal restaurant.

This is about you.

If you want to unleash your restaurant, you will have to face some dark places that you have ignored. You'll have to ask yourself those questions that you have avoided.

If there are times while you're reading and you get uncomfortable, that's good. Being comfortable is why you are where you are in life and business.

They say the truth will set you free, but first, it will piss you off.

Ready to get pissed off?

*"I don't fix restaurant problems;
I fix the mindset that created
the problem in the first place.
Once you fix that the problems
seem to fix themselves."*

Donald Burns, The Restaurant Coach™

You Are Here

Have you ever looked at the map at a mall and found that little dot that said: "you are here"?

I have some good news and bad news for you.

The bad news: Your restaurant is what you think it should be. That's exactly where you are right now. You are where you thought you should be. What you think you are, you become.

The good news: When you change your mindset, you change your restaurant

*...and your **life**.*

If you thought this was going to be your typical "how to run a restaurant" type of book, sorry to let you down. We are going to discuss the real issues holding your restaurant back from reaching its true potential...You.

That 3-pound piece of grey matter that sits atop your neck nestled in between your ears is capable of amazing things. It's also the thing that holds you back. It means well (most of the time). It's just that you let the reptilian part of your brain do the driving more than you should. Inside that beautiful brain are some outdated beliefs, rituals, and habits, keeping you stuck in mental quicksand. Those things are like an old software program running in the background. You don't notice them and the negative impact they have upon your restaurant and your life. It is time to update your mental management operating system.

The Habit Trap

We like to think we make every decision throughout the day. The reality is that **40-45%**

of those things, you call "decisions" are habits that are buried in the oldest part of your brain called the basal ganglia (that reptilian part).

Just like anything, we have good habits, and we have some bad habits. Here are a few that impact your restaurant more than you realize:

- Complaining
- Gossip
- Talking down to people
- Having cliques
- Uncontrolled outbursts
- Isolating yourself
- Being late
- Being messy
- Inefficiency
- Emotional reactivity to text or emails
- Poor communication
- Not recharging/taking strategic breaks
- Lack of self-care
- Not planning the day/week
- Playing the martyr
- Managing in reaction mode
- Lack of follow-through
- Inconsistency

HOW ARE HABITS FORMED?

Habits are formed when actions are tied to a trigger by consistent repetition. When the trigger happens, you have an automatic urge to act.

For example:
* When you wake up (trigger), you start the coffee machine (habit).
* When you get to work (trigger), you check your email (habit).
* When you get stressed (trigger), you yell at your team (habit).

Our lives are filled with these trigger-habit combos, often without our being aware of them. If you drive home from work every day following the same route, you probably often drive by habit, making turns without thinking about it, because of constant repetition.

How does this happen?

1. Consistent repetition over the years. *Think of it like this; walking on the rug in the same way until you start to see a path.*
2. You start with actions performed very consciously at first before they were a habit. Gradually, they became more automatic and less conscious. *All habits are born from thought.*
3. There is a feedback loop that helped us repeat the habit. For example, if you are stressed and eat junk food, you might get pleasure (positive feedback), and if you don't eat junk food, you remain stressed (negative feedback). So, positive feedback for indulging an urge makes you want to do it repeatedly. Negative feedback for not indulging makes you not want to do it repeatedly.

Whenever the trigger happens, it leads to the formation of a habit.
When you change the trigger, you can change the habit.

Why Change is So Difficult

You know, deep down you should make changes in your restaurant.

Why don't you?

Change is a fickle thing. While it calls to us to embrace it, it is also is quite resistant to being caught. Change is a hypocrite. When you try to make changes in your life and your restaurant, it pushes back. Why?

Negative habits are resistant to change.

Those habits you and your team have run deep, and it will take more than a memo or a one-hour workshop to evict them. Habits are at the foundation of change theory. To be able to conquer them, you have to first understand why change is so hard to achieve, which I'll lead into monkeys and food. Seriously.

The Monkey Mindset

Some of the Pararescuemen stationed in the Philippines tell the story of how hunters catch a monkey; they use a strategy that understands the monkey's behavior patterns. These patterns sometimes work against the monkey's best interests *(of course you never work against your own best interests, do you?)*

A hunter takes a jar with an opening slightly larger than a monkey's hand. He ties a rope around the neck of it using a knot, called a monkey's knot (I know very original) which is a cradle of the rope around the jar. The hunter places some food in the glass jar, like rice or a banana.

The monkey reaches his hand into the jar, grabs the food, making a fist with his paw. Now, the monkey's dilemma: the monkey cannot get his hand out of the jar unless he drops the food. The neck of the jar is not wide enough. Of course, the monkey could drop the food and easily get his hand out, but he won't. His Monkey Mindset won't let him! Despite having the ability to escape, he doesn't — he holds his hand tight around the food screaming until a hunter throws a net over the monkey and captures him.

Have you ever held onto something that you should've let go?

Many people don't know when to let go and move on. This can happen a lot in restaurants; when one holds something beyond when they should let go, and move on. Perhaps you have some staff you feel, deep down, you should let go. You still hold onto them like that monkey with his hand around the banana...screaming about the problems they cause and the drama they create, when all you have to do is open your hand and free yourself.

Do you have some personal habits you are holding onto that you should let go? *Come on, be honest with yourself!*

Is it hard to let them go? Yes. Is it required if you ever are going to grow yourself and your business? Absolutely!

Here are three obstacles sabotaging your efforts.

3 Reasons You Don't Change

1. FEAR

Fear; real or imaginary is a powerful enemy to change. Fear keeps us immobilized and stuck in situations that we know; deep down, we should change.

Marketers know that, and they use fear as a tool to get us to buy all kind of things we don't need. Do you allow fear to use you, or do you use fear to move into action?

Fear of the unknown is ever-present and can be paralyzing if we allow it.

Why don't you train your team more?

Fear says, "If I invest in training them more and they get better skills, they will take those skills to another restaurant."

False.

The *real* fear you must have is that if you do **not** invest in your team to elevate your food, service, marketing, and leadership, then you will not improve, and you will be stuck. Your competition will be the one who adapts, outperforms, outsells, out markest, and out trains you.

Fear is natural and hard-wired into our brains as a survival mechanism. Fear needs to be acknowledged and respected. It does not have to be obeyed. Face your fears, address them, and then do the opposite of what fear suggests. "Okay, I can see where investing in training the team is risky, and there is a chance that some will take those skills and leave to another restaurant. Those that stay will become better, and that will elevate the entire brand."

2. COMFORT ZONE

Being comfortable is dangerous. When you are in your comfort zone, you are vulnerable. If you are not adapting to keep pace or better yet, stay innovative and ahead of the pack, you'll quickly find yourself displaced in your market.

Your comfort zone is a place where bad habits hang out. They're like old friends, and no one wants to get rid of an old friend, especially if you've known them since childhood. Some of those habits have been living up in your head for a long time, rent-free. It's time to start writing some eviction notices.

3. FALSE EXPECTATIONS

You have what is known as the fortune teller syndrome. You already have a preconceived notion that it will *not* work out. This is also known as being a pessimist. You can usually tell if someone suffers from this by the language they use. Do any of these statements sound familiar:

We tried that before. *(Really, how many times?)*

That won't work in our market. *(Do you have data and research to back that up?)*

We've always done it like this. *(That might be the problem.)*

This fortune teller syndrome is what psychologists call **negativity bias**. Our minds are wired to help us survive and adapt. Unfortunately, some of that wiring is not conducive to helping you grow your business. Negativity bias is when your mind reacts to bad things stronger than it does towards the good. It takes five positive comments to override every negative one.

The good news is that now you know. Having inside information on how your brain is wired helps create change. When you are aware of something like negativity bias, you have a choice. You can choose to accept it or choose a different path. That's the amazing thing about free will; you have a choice.

Now that you understand some of the things holding you back from making the changes you need let's explore how to implement change in your life

...and your restaurant.

The 3 P's to Making Change Happen

PURPOSE

Knowing your purpose, vision, mission, or why you need to change is powerful. If you know why the how is easy. The biggest obstacle is not connecting to a powerful enough why. Your purpose has to be connected to emotions. You can think of lots of logical reasons why you should change. Logic does not move us to take action.

Let's look at a common change many people struggle with: going to the gym.

On the surface, you can think of a dozen reasons why you should go.

- You'll feel better.
- You'll have more energy.
- You'll be healthier.

Why do most people not commit and take action? Many have not tapped into the emotions of what they get as a result of going to the gym. Think about the feelings you get after working out. Confidence. Happy. Calm. Love. Yes, love because taking time to take care of yourself is love.

When you tap into emotions, you tap into your ultimate power source.

PERSISTENCE

Change will push back. That sweet, soft voice of your comfort zone will come calling. You have to be committed to staying the course. This is especially difficult for restaurants because while you might be extremely committed and dedicated to seeing these changes take place in your business, other people on your team might not share the same enthusiasm. If you've tapped into a strong why you will be able to weather the storm of negativity and doubt from your team.

Persistence also means being adaptable and making adjustments as needed. Of course, not everything goes as planned. Be ready for obstacles to rise and challenge you. Thinking ahead and having contingency plans are the best way to circumvent these occurrences.

In neuro-linguistic programming (NLP) there is a presupposition (guiding principle) that states, "If something doesn't work, try something else. If that doesn't work, try something else. If that doesn't work, try something else."

Get the hint? Too many times, we try to implement change and give up too easily.

PATIENCE

Back in the 1950s, there was a plastic surgeon named Maxwell Maltz, who was fascinated by human behavior. Maltz discovered that it took a patient 21 days to get used to seeing their new face after surgery. This is where the famous 21 Days to Break a Habit Myth started.

The truth is, on average, it takes more than two months before a new habit or change becomes automatic. *In most cases, 66 days to be exact.* Can you see where a lot of people give up too easily when they don't see their new behavior take effect after only 21 days? For some people, it may take even longer.

Phillippa Lally is a health psychology researcher at University College London. She did a study published in the European Journal of Social Psychology, that showed it took anywhere from 18 days to 254 days for people to form a new habit. Habits truly do make and break restaurants. Habits are a reflection of the standards set for the brand. It's in things we see like the way they answer the phone, greet a guest, serve a drink, plate an entrée, treat each other, clean the bathroom, present the check, and how they say goodbye.

It's also in the things we might not notice like updating cost, managing budgets, training, team communication, hiring, and employee appreciation. Some habits are easy to start, like showing appreciation daily. It's as simple as walking up to someone on your team or a guest and saying just two words… **thank you**.

If you want your restaurant to stand out and excel, then developing positive habits is a necessity. Aristotle said it best, *"We are what we repeatedly do. Excellence, then, is not an act, but a habit."*

Where is Your Map?

When I was in the USAF Pararescue teams, we would be "inserted" or dropped off in scenarios that most of the time was not like we had discussed. Very similar to the day-to-day situations most restaurants face. You started with a damn good plan and then, the day hits and your damn good plan turns to a bad day faster than big-screen TVs sell on Black Friday. Does it change?

Not really.

What does change is how you deal with it.

First, we need to figure out where we are and where we want to go. I call this your M.A.P. or Massive Action Plan. That old cliché is correct, "if you fail to plan, then you are planning to fail."

I am shocked by the number of restaurants that do not have a Massive Action Plan for their business or their life. They live in pure day-to-day reaction to what is going on around them. In the Spec Ops world, if you did not have a solid plan and work through several contingency plans as well, people died. Restaurants might not be so life-and-death on the surface. However, not having a plan and making adjustments is the same as slowly bleeding to death internally. Why do so many restaurants fail? Much of it is due to piss poor planning. Remember these words from George S. Patton:

> *"A good plan violently executed now is better than a perfect plan executed next week."*

If you are not getting the results that you want for your restaurant and your life, then it's time to get busy creating a new Massive Action Plan or map. Time to throw out those old maps and routines (habits) you have clung to like a security blanket. We are heading into new territory. There are no road signs where we are going. This is an uncharted area for many. Your comfort zone will call you and ask you to come back. Ignore the call because it has nothing to offer you only the same nonexistent results you were getting before. Don't worry; I'll be your guide on this journey. **You are going to have to trust me.** I will push you and hit those buttons that trigger: fear, anxiety, doubt, and at times, anger. I am doing this to challenge your old view and help you see a new path.

Tools are Only Potential

Imagine a hammer sitting on a counter. Would you call it a tool? It is only when you pick it up and use it. Just sitting there, it's only a *potential* tool. Once you pick it up now, you can use it as a tool. That tool can also be applied for good or bad. Drive a nail into a wall to build a house, good. Use it to hit someone in the head out of anger, bad.

Throughout this book, I will drop all kinds of potential tools right in your lap (*in fact, I will repeat them a few times to make sure you get the message*). It will be on you to pick them up and apply them for either good or bad. Some of the psychological tools in these pages can be used to influence your team, or they can be used to change yourself. I am expecting you are reading this because you have integrity. Using these tools to improve yourself, your team, and if your restaurant is on that path, those with integrity will follow. Those less scrupulous people can find some quick impact and get some temporary results. When you pack these tools with bad intentions, you won't last long in this business. That is a guarantee.

As I mentioned earlier, to get new results, you sometimes have to do something you've never done to get something you've never had. You have been doing the same thing over and over for years (creating unconscious habits). Time to break free and pull away from your normal patterns. Time to learn some new things.

The minute you stop learning, you start dying.

To be successful, you need the right knowledge. Then you need to be relentless in applying that knowledge through the right actions. *Consistently.*

Don't talk about it.

Fucking do something with it!

Please, don't get caught up in the perfection excuse! So many people in the restaurant industry love to throw out the "I'm a perfectionist" line. *Bullshit.* Perfection is not truly attainable, and if you ever did hit that mark, *what then?* Where do you go after it's perfect?

How many times have you been half-way through a great podcast, an amazing blog post, or attended a seminar and had some inspiration to get up and do something? What happened next? If you're like many people, you didn't do shit. You let those intense feelings get all stirred up and failed to take action! Or, you did one or two things, and then you stopped. That is the habit of losers. Start and stop. Then they see the next shiny object, and they try that. Start and stop. No commitment to taking consistent action. Just like the boy who cried wolf. All talk. No results.

Nothing will ever change in your life or for your restaurant until you take action consistency and follow through on your M.A.P. That's why you need it. It is your guide. Your core values are your compass. You need to consider one last thing before you get busy taking the tools in this book and applying them.

Lose Your Mind

Do you hear those voices in your head?

"What voices?"

We all have this committee in our head with a role to stop us from doing things and start to question what we are about to do. This voice was created as a survival tool so the human race could adapt to some pretty harsh environments. These remnants of our reptilian brain can become the roadblock to getting the restaurant and life we desire.

They mean well. But are full of shit.

These voices throw out two completely different points of view that would surely confuse most: the past and the future.

THE PAST

The events from years ago come flashing into your head like an old 8mm movie. Remember when that one kid stole some steaks from the cooler? How about when that guy you thought was a great hire didn't show up on the first day? Like it or not, you might say you have forgotten the past until that committee in your head starts to see a sign that you are heading down what they think is a familiar road. As soon as that happens, watch out for the roadblocks!

The past hurts. Second-guessing, insecurities, blame, shame, and judgments all come forward to make their case. The problem is, if your committee went to a real court, they would lose on circumstantial evidence. Your head's full of hearsay.

Better known as bullshit.

THE FUTURE

The committee in your brain also plays fortune teller. "Look into the crystal ball, and we'll tell you exactly what's going to happen." If you really could predict the future, you would know exactly what the next line in this book would be, right?

When the "future committee" gets in on your decision making, they play the gloom and doom angle. In their defense, they are trying to protect you. However, they can be a little overprotective.

Worst-case scenarios, false premonitions, doubt, distrust, lack of confidence, and a creative storytelling ability that would make Stephen King jealous are what show up when these voices take over. The truth is, what you make up in your mind is never as bad as you imagined it would be.

And if it is, so what? You deal with it because you can't change events only how you respond to events.

THE BIASES THAT HOLD YOU BACK

Then when something appears to be similar to a past event, we lump the experience into the same category and say something like, "see, I knew that was going to happen." That is actually what psychologists call hind-site bias.

The human brain has been evolving a long time, and it's wired to do one thing extremely well, keep you alive. Place your hand on something hot, and your brain jumps into action to pull your hand away. You don't even have time to think about it. Action and reaction. It also has some cool shortcuts programmed to give you an edge in the real world. If you didn't have a memory, then every time you approached a door, you would have to stop and assess the situation to determine what the hell this rectangular object is between rooms. There is also some faulty wiring up there as well. Say hello to some things known as cognitive biases.

We live in a world where millions of bits of information are coming at us every second. To process everything, we tend to create mental shortcuts. Our brains often use shortcuts to help us. These shortcuts are called heuristics. These mental shortcuts are incredibly useful, and they're quite accurate.

Unfortunately for us, heuristics aren't infallible.

Sometimes things aren't exactly as they appear on the surface (for example, a common situation has been slightly changed or is unique). In these instances, relying on heuristics can seriously hurt us and cause us to make bad decisions. When our heuristics fail to produce a correct judgment, the result is a cognitive bias – which is the tendency to draw an incorrect conclusion in a certain circumstance based on cognitive factors. Cognitive biases can affect us in all aspects of life; from shopping to relationships, from jury verdicts to job interviews. Cognitive biases are especially important for those in the restaurant industry, whose main goal should be to think as rationally and logically as possible to find the true vision of a business.

Therefore, an awareness of the heuristics your brain uses and the cognitive biases they can cause is imperative if you want to be a successful restaurateur or operator. Every cognitive bias is there for a reason — primarily to save our brains time or energy. Some of them are like bad wiring that most people are unaware they have. There are around 175 cognitive biases that we use.

Let's cover the most popular ones you will need to be aware of and manage like a professional in the foodservice industry.

Confirmation Bias

This occurs when you warp data to fit or support your existing beliefs or expectations. The effects are often found in religion, politics, and I see it being prevalent in restaurants.

Why does that matter? Because an inability to look outside of your existing belief systems will vastly limit your ability to grow and improve, both in business and in life. We need to consider more possibilities and be more open to other ways to do things. There are a lot of different equations that you can use to reach the end goal. Sure $50 + 25 + 25 = 100$. They are also many, many other ways to get that same solution.

The Dunning–Kruger Effect

A cognitive bias wherein relatively unskilled individuals suffer from illusory superiority, mistakenly assessing their ability to be much higher than is accurate. People think they are much better than they are.

Like the restaurant that thinks they serve great food, yet their online reviews tell a different story. There is a difference between being cocky and being confident.

Cocky people talk a good game while confident people deliver results.

Status Quo Bias

The "Status Quo" bias is very similar to loss-aversion bias, where people prefer to avoid losses instead of acquiring gains. An example would be the restaurant owner who knows they should change their menu. However, the fear of losing customers is greater than the gain of acquiring new customers and more business.

Zero-Risk Bias

The preference to reduce a small risk to zero versus achieving a greater reduction in greater risk. This plays to the desire to have complete control over a single, more minor outcome, over the desire for more (however not certain) control over an unpredictable outcome. In the restaurant world, this is the restaurant owner, manager, or chef who thinks beating up a vendor on pricing is controlling their food cost.

They focus on price because they feel they have control over that by getting the "lowest price." The reality is that they focus so much on a minor thing that they do not pay attention to their theoretical food cost (costing out their menu), production waste or doing a menu analysis to understand what the customer is buying.

Blind-Spot Bias
Failing to recognize your own cognitive biases is a bias itself.

People notice cognitive and negative biases much more in others than in themselves.

Overconfidence Bias
The overconfidence effect is a well-established bias in which a person's subjective confidence in his or her judgments is reliably greater than the objective accuracy of those judgments, especially when confidence is relatively high. Overconfidence is one example of a miscalculation of probabilities.

Overconfidence has been defined in three distinct ways:

1. Overestimation of one's actual performance;
2. Over placement of one's performance relative to others; and
3. Overprecision in expressing unwarranted certainty in the accuracy of one's beliefs, you bought your own bullshit story.

Illusion of Control
Many times, the manager has never been trained on how to accurately calculate food cost, analyze menus, or manage food production, so they focus on the one thing they feel they have an impact on, pricing. Control is an illusion, yet many cling to it like a security blanket. The illusion of control describes the tendency for people to behave as if they might have some control when, in fact, they have none.

Parkinson's Law
Be aware of Parkinson's Law, which states, "Work expands to fill the time available for its completion." There's some truth in this – if you schedule two hours for an activity, then you'll often find that it takes two hours to do. However, if you only give yourself an hour, chances are you'll be more focused

and finish it in the allotted time. Use this to give yourself tighter deadlines, and more efficient use with your precious time.

Planning Fallacy

This one tends to be one of the cognitive biases that trips me up. The planning fallacy is a phenomenon in which predictions about how much time will be needed to complete a future task display an optimism bias and underestimate the time needed. We tend to think we can get a project done far sooner than it ultimately takes.

You can use these cognitive biases as an excuse to stay stuck and stay average. Or, you can drop the bullshit and admit the root cause of your problems.

Overthinking.

The reason you may not be getting things done and moving your restaurant forward is that you are standing at the crossroads of **should** and **must**; thinking way too much. Hesitation and overthinking are chains holding you stuck. What's the cure?

Stop thinking and start doing!

Okay. Get doing.

Check the MAP

The year was 1986. I was in the rugged mountains of Northern Wales. I was on a navigation exercise with my team of Pararescue operatives.

Now Wales is both beauty and the beast. The mountains are breathtaking, and the weather can turn very quickly with wind and rain that can come in fast. So, fast that many mountaineers get caught blindsided and become victims of the elements. I was taking the lead and heading for a small mountain shelter that was on the map. Wales places many of these shelters among the mountains to provide a safe refuge for those caught in bad weather. I was certain of my course. I was tired and knew I was headed in the right direction. The rain was so heavy that it became hard to check the surroundings and the night had come in as well. My teammate behind me questioned my direction. "Wait." He said. "We need to check the map." It's right up at the top of this ridge I assured. "Wait. Check the map." No. It's right there. Then he grabbed me and stopped me. "Stop being a stubborn ass and check the damn map." Okay. We stopped and pulled out the map and compass.

Sure, enough I was a few degrees off course…okay more like 90 degrees. The shelter was 500 feet to the right.

We grabbed up the map and compass we had out, and by accident, I kicked over a big rock. I heard it roll for a second and then nothing. I turned my headlamp toward the nothingness and saw I was three steps from walking straight off a 1000-foot ravine. My teammate saved my life that day. He saved me from my stubbornness and inability to listen. *Have you ever done that?* Have you been so sure that you keep going without checking your bearings? That's why having a MAP, and a compass is so critical. I use my map or Massive Action Plan as my guide to where I am going. Remember that if you don't care where you are going, then any road will get you there. My compass makes sure I act in congruence with my actions, and that compass is my core values. They keep me on my path, and I carry them with me.

CULTURE

"Culture flows down, not up in your restaurant. Culture starts with you!

Donald Burns, The Restaurant Coach™

The River of Culture

How Great Restaurants Control the Flow

Culture.

This is a word we throw around in the restaurant industry quite often. It's one of those popular buzzwords we tend to use to sound cool, but many of us don't know what it means.

Let's take a journey down the river of culture to understand better where culture starts, how it grows, what blocks it, and how you can keep the flow going. Culture is truly like a river in the sense that its final destination is the guest. You always want to begin with the end in mind.

THE SOURCE

The start of the river is you. You… the owner, operator, or chef running the restaurant. You are the creator and source of culture in your brand. Now, if that statement does not make you feel a little uncomfortable, then you don't understand the power that culture has.

What exactly is culture?

If we were looking at a textbook definition, it would say: *"Culture is a system of shared beliefs, values, customs, and behaviors that members of a group use to cope with their world and with one another that is passed down from generation to generation through learning."*

Yipes! Sounds a little intense and boring. How about this: *"Culture is emotional energy that is created and nurtured through habits, learning, sharing, structure, and connection."*

Write this down… **Culture is learned.**

All restaurants have a culture whether they know it or not. When you get a group of people together, a culture within that group will develop. It's a natural law. If you don't take an active role in the creation of that culture, you're very likely to get one that you don't want.

To take no action *is* an action.

The strength of any river is dictated by its source of water. In the case of your culture, it's the energy that you put in. As the leader, you set the tone and the tempo of the culture within your restaurant. Everything you are contributes to the energy source. Like it or not, your culture and your restaurant are a reflection of who you are.

HOW IT GROWS

As a river flows, it constantly picks up more sources of water. Many restaurant owners believe that creating a culture is a one-time event. Without consistently controlling what sources are feeding into your river, it could soon go out of control like a flash flood. And once you lose control of your culture, it's very difficult to get it back.

Civil engineers monitor rivers and take proactive steps to control the speed and force of the water. That's your job as an owner or operator. Control the flow. Set the expectations. Monitor and make adjustments as you need.

"If you don't take an active role in the creation of your restaurant culture, you're likely to get one that you don't want."

You provide the energy and direction of the culture by being a living example of what your culture is. One of the traits of culture is, it is shared. The best thing you can do to ensure its longevity is simple: raise your standards and never compromise them. Too many people are afraid to do this in their restaurants and settle for mediocrity instead.

If you truly want to improve your restaurant, start right now. You have the power. Determine what you will no longer tolerate. Make a stand for who you are and what your restaurant is all about.

WHO BLOCKS IT

Items will fall into your river and attempt to obstruct its flow. These 'items' are people who are resistant to change and comfortable with mediocrity. The funny thing is, when you try to change something, change will push back. For some people, push back is enough to get them to do the one thing they should never do, lower their standards.

What do you do when a tree falls into a river and blocks its flow? Get an ax and remove it. The biggest obstacle in the river of culture is negativity.

Negativity breeds complacency.

Complacency invites mediocrity.

Mediocrity is death to your restaurant.

If there are negative people within your organization who are affecting your culture, you need to remove them. Immediately. Like today.

Now some of you might say, "I can't. They are a workhorse." Not if they are poisoning your culture. In business, you have assets and liabilities. Lest you forget that your job as an owner or operator is to maximize and increase your assets while reducing or eliminating your liabilities. Which side of the equation do you think negative people fall on? They are cancer in your business and are slowly driving away your top talent and your guests. When a doctor finds a cancer tumor, what do they do? They cut it the fuck out!

Contrary to popular opinion, it was Charles Dickens, and not Spock in *Star Trek II: The Wrath of Khan* who said, *"The needs of the many outweigh the needs of the few."* As the architect of culture, your job is to remove items that slow down the flow.

HOW TO KEEP IT GOING

Restaurants are like a living thing. They have good days and bad days. They grow. They mature. They undergo different phases of growth and change.

Every phase in your restaurant's life will require a different you.

You are the catalyst for change and culture. Restaurants get better when the people in them become better, and that starts with you becoming a better leader.

The Internet is such an amazing source of information if you are willing to take advantage of it. There are unlimited online courses and resources that create learning opportunities 24/7. Most are mobile compatible, which means you can access them from any Internet device, so there's no real excuse for not learning and becoming more of the leader you can be.

Make a decision right now to be better and to maximize your potential. A lot of people know what they should do to build a stronger restaurant. Eat better. Sleep better. Read more. Communicate more. Learn more. However, few ever take action. Ego, pride, and denial keep restaurants stuck in the cult of mediocrity. You have the power to escape that if you choose to.

THE END OF THE RIVER

At the end of our river of culture is the guest. Great cultures transform guest experiences into memories. Great cultures create raving fans that are brand loyal. Great cultures have low turnover and higher employee engagement. Great cultures endure the ups and downs of economic markets. Great cultures endure. Great cultures become iconic. Great cultures are built.

Great cultures start, and end, with you.

A Restaurant Coach™ Tip: Honor Your Core Values.

When you honor your core values, you honor your true self. When you live by a clear set of values, it is easier to align your life with your goals. When you are living your core values with authenticity and integrity, you are a leader people will want to work for and follow.

How Core Values Impact Your Restaurant's Culture

Caravelle

"I'm knackered. I don't know how to get people to our place? We are busy for brunch and buggered on the weekdays."

The heavy Australian accent makes it a challenge for me. Zim Sutton owns a small cafe in Barcelona, Spain named Caravelle. He is a stranger in a strange land. The Australian chef lived in England where he and a business partner owned a gastropub that served a blend of Australian and British food with a little Mediterranean flair thrown in. He sold his business in 2011 and came down to Barcelona for a break. Once there, the energy of the area revived his passion for the business. In 2012 they opened their restaurant in the heart of Barcelona on Carrer del Pintor Fortuny. A year later and he is struggling. He's read some of my blogs and reaches out for help.

This is my first Skype Video Coaching Call with him and his wife, Poppy. I can see the stress on his face. Zim is a dead ringer for actor Colin Farrell. Poppy smiles to hide it, however, the way she is sitting and keeps looking away, tells me she is stressed too. On a phone call, you might be able to get by with not telling me the truth. In a video call, I can see it for myself. Trust me that body language reveals more than words ever could. First things first. I have to determine where his business is. This requires building rapport in the coaching process to create trust. Just like any great relationship, you have to trust that your coach is looking out for your best interests. When I get these calls, I know things are worse than they tell me.

We jump right in.

Zim is an incredible chef with uncompromising standards. That's good and bad. Some chefs cannot get past the food part and understand that this is a business. He is firm on his philosophy of, "If we can make it, we don't buy it." Hardcore. I respect that.

Brunch took off as soon as they opened. Caravelle's eclectic menu is filled with tasty creations that have lured tourists and locals alike to the small cafe. Weekdays are a bust. Like many restaurants that struggle they try the "be everything to everyone" mentality and turn it into a brunch fest all day, every day. All owners have a driving question that they ask themselves often. The questions you ask yourself on a habitual basis are the foundation of the results you see. If you want better results, you need to ask yourself better quality questions.

Zim's primary question at the time was, "how do we brunch it the fuck up?" The problem with the question you ask yourself is that you usually get what you ask for. The lines between brunch and dinner became blurred. Soon, it became a monster out of control — time to ask better questions.

"So, Zim, what is Caravelle at its essence? What are your core values?"

"Shit. I guess we haven't thought about it." Zim replies.

I said, "Let's start there."

Over the next few video calls, we drilled down to what Caravelle was to him and Poppy. They were about family, fresh, made in house, local, and especially fun. Brunch had become anything but fun — time to make some changes. Taco Sundays became a big hit along with gourmet burgers. Zim's passion for making as much as he could in house lead to house-made hot sauce, pickles, salsas, craft sodas, and beer.

After the foundation of core values is firmly set, we start to frame out the brand with systems, team, and the menu. Zim had a graphic designer give their logo a fresh look, and he reduced the menu to his greatest hits. Most menus can be a paradox of choice for the guests with so many options that making a decision becomes a stressful situation. Restaurants that become outstanding make the guest experience enjoyable and effortless. Trust me; effortless is not easy. It takes more planning and training to pull it off. When you do, your guests will wonder how you make it all look so easy.

That's the goal.

When we're putting up the foundation, we dig into the dynamics of your team. I'm not talking about skill, it's all about personality, and more specifically, it's behavior. Behavior does predict performance. Just because a guy came from a great restaurant, does not guarantee he'll be great in your restaurant. You'll need to look beyond the words on the resume. I often tell people when looking at that hyped-up piece of paper, "This tells me where you've worked, it doesn't tell me how you work, or how you'll mesh with the team." Zim hired a young chef that had talent. He also had a bad attitude. The kid didn't seem to understand that it was Zim's restaurant and his brand.

Zim was very apprehensive about getting rid of the young chef since he just was about to have his second child and feared that firing the kid would mean he'd have to go back to working in his restaurant instead of on his restaurant. Sometimes you have to regroup and not by choice. The young chef was subversive and pitted the staff to walk out. Half of the kitchen left. With anything that comes at you, there is a learning opportunity. Refocused menus and some new blood in the kitchen had started to dial in the restaurant to match the core values and the real vision for Caravelle.

Caravelle's social media had lacked focus. Now with the firmly established values, revised brand image, and new menu, it was time to get busy making noise on the internet. More pictures of people that convey the core values. More education about ingredients that show value and position the brand to stand out. More posts across all social media channels. More of telling the world what Caravelle was all about...fun.

Some restaurant coaching clients have been with me for years. Some stay till they can get their momentum going. You don't forget your first kiss in your youth. Some things stay with you for life. Caravelle was my first international client, and to this day, one I am proud and honored to have coached. Zim sent me an email about six months after our coaching time was over and I keep it printed out in my office to remind myself that core values are always the foundation to any brand that wants to aim for outstanding.

"Once we worked out our core values with Donald, we used that as a platform to base everything on, from our menu design, hiring policy, and especially our social media which really focused our message, helping us to engage with our customers properly. He helped put together an action plan to tighten our systems and get our staff more productive. Just having Donald to bounce ideas off each week gave us the confidence to take Caravelle to the level we wanted it to be."

Zim Sutton
Caravelle
Barcelona, Spain
9/24/2014

It is estimated that every year, approximately 43,000 new restaurants open. By the 3rd year, 50% will be gone.

The majority of those go out of business as a result of poor planning or poor management. Sadly, most of these failed businesses could have been saved. The shattered dreams and lives of the owners, managers, and employees could have turned out better… tweaked into success, just like Caravelle.

One thousand details go into opening a restaurant. However, the most important decision a restaurant has to make is their brand identity. If you search in Amazon the number of books on "branding," it will return more search results than restaurants in your state!

As a restaurant coach, I work with over 500 restaurants a year (through workshops, seminars, webinars, online courses, and my coaching programs). When you work with that many restaurants, you tend to see patterns of success and patterns of failure. I've seen firsthand the main reason that restaurants get off-track. If I had to list the top three reasons, it would look like this:

3. A failed menu
2. A failed brand

And the number one reason?

1. A failure of core values.

"It's not hard to make decisions when you know what your core values are."

-Roy Disney

Disney was right. Core values build your restaurant's culture, and your culture is the foundation of your brand. But what are company core values? Why are they so important?

Digging into Your Restaurant's Core Values

Core values support the vision your restaurant stands for. They are essential to your brand identity because they lay out the principles, beliefs, and philosophies of what is most important to you. Many restaurants focus only on the mechanics of service or on hiring a talented chef. While these are important, if you want to *thrive* and not just *survive,* establishing strong core values will provide an edge over your competition.

Core values help restaurants in the decision-making process and with restaurant management. For example, if one of your core values is to stand behind the quality of your products, any products not reaching a satisfactory standard are automatically not served. Imagine a culinary team and service team that stood behind and enforced core values and refused to serve substandard food to a guest. If you adopted this core value, would it decrease guest complaints?

Of course.

Having solid core values helps to educate your customers about your restaurant branding and what you stand for. In this highly competitive industry, having a strong set of core values sets your brand apart. Take a look at Danny Meyers and his Union Square Hospitality Group. Danny goes out of his way to educate and inform the public of his company's core values. Many successful restaurateurs have adopted his Enlightened Hospitality model.

Core values become a primary recruiting and retention tool. When you establish a solid set of core values in the restaurant, you will see a dramatic change in the people drawn to your culture.

How to Establish Your Core Values and Improve Your Culture

How do you find the right core values for your restaurant?

Many restaurants make the mistake of picking core values out of thin air and trying to make them fit into their organization. Unfortunately, core values are not a one-size-fits-all kind of thing. As the owner or leader, they have to resonate with *you* first. Remember, culture flows down, not up.

Your restaurant culture starts with you.

Core values only work in a restaurant when the leader *lives them,* rather than just talking about them. Your core values have to come from within. They have to mean something to you. Here's an easy exercise to help you get on track.

1. Start a list of core values that might resonate with you. Think of things like community, charity, authentic, local, fresh, honesty, integrity, hospitality, creative, dependability, family, adaptability, quality, consistency, teamwork, credibility, respect. Get a good list of about 20 to 40 core values that pop into your head without too much thought.
2. Now look at that list and start highlighting the ones that stand out to you. These will be values that make a connection deep inside you. This becomes your core values list. You should end up with 1 to 8.

SECOND EDITION NOTE:

I used to say that you could have up to 8 core values for your brand. Over the last year, that has changed when I found that people cannot remember that many. So, now my philosophy is to keep it to three or four max! Take those three or four and type them up and put them in places where you and your employees can be reminded of what truly inspires and drives you. The best way to write them out is to make a short sentence for value to make them easier to remember.

Here are mine for The Restaurant Coach™ brand:

1. **Be creative.**
2. **Have an impact.**
3. **Embrace Kaizen.**

One of the most important roles as a restaurant owner or operator is to get on your soapbox and preach your company's core values every single day to your team.

Core values are the foundation of your restaurant culture. Core values do more than promote ethical business practices. They act as a map for decision-making criteria that your managers and employees will use to guide their actions. The more strongly defined the core values, the more likely that this value system will serve as a code of conduct. That promotes and guides strategically aligned behaviors that reinforce your brand identity.

Restaurants with strong cultures that share common core values will have happier employees. Happier employees make businesses more productive. There is empirical research that suggests core values directly correlate with restaurant performance and profitability. Connecting with your restaurant's core values is a step towards building a better restaurant brand.

I keep my list of core values on my phone and look at it every morning to make sure I'm in line and acting in congruence with those values as I approach business throughout the day. If I face a difficult situation, sometimes I pull the list out to make sure I'm living my truth, my values as I see them. It's helped me make much better decisions when I am in alignment with the core values that resonate deep within me.

Don't just preach it... live it.

Restaurant Coach™ Private Session: About Those Core Values

I want you to think about your core values. You know what those things are. You see those posters on walls in most companies or even in your restaurant.

Here's the thing. Most of those fancy core values posters are just bullshit because the people who I wrote them don't believe them. They are more like a list of wishful thinking. I will also tell you that if you can dig deep and come up with 3-4 solid core values that truly resonate with your heart and soul, you'll be on the path to a better restaurant. Now, don't pick words that sound good or are the "right ones." Core values have to be something that you, as the leader, can live each day as an example. They also have to be described as an action, not just a single word. It's not integrity, it's always doing the right thing, all the time. It's not innovation; it's looking at problems differently. It's not hospitality; it's connecting with people from the heart. Do you see the difference? Words by themselves have so many different meanings, so you need to clarify the emotion behind the words.

"Restaurants become better when the people in them become better people."

Donald Burns, The Restaurant Coach™

Build Your Culture, Build Your Brand

Bigfoot. The Loch Ness Monster. Restaurant Culture.

What do these three have in common?

They are all elusive creatures that many search for, only to come away empty-handed. While Bigfoot and the Loch Ness Monster may be mythical folklore, culture is very real. It has a bigger impact on your restaurant brand than most can imagine. Culture is the glue that holds your guests to your brand. Some restaurants have a lot of "brand stickiness," and their guests stay loyal through the years.

Others have a culture that has the stickiness of a post-it-note.

Culture is Like a Child

You've invested a lot of time, energy, and resources to develop your menu. You need to have that same mindset when it comes to culture. Your restaurant's culture is a living thing that needs to be nurtured and carefully groomed. Think of culture like the growth cycle of a person. When you were young, your parents molded you about right and wrong, good and bad, what was and was not acceptable in their house.

Your restaurant's culture is the same.

When you start, it's like a child that will try to get away with as much as it can — time to tighten the reins and set the tone. Things go good for a while until they hit the teens. Then your culture will become rebellious and will want to see how far they can push. *What you put up with, you end up with.*

You have to watch the growth of your culture carefully, that's your duty as an owner or operator. Too many leave it to its own and then complain because their restaurant now runs them.

Building Culture

So, if culture is so important, why do fewer than 10% of restaurants build a successful one? Like a lot of things in the restaurant industry, you need a solid recipe.

Let's create the perfect culture recipe:

Step 1: Start with your Core Values

If you don't know what you stand for, you'll fall for anything. Core values are the foundation of your brand. When you know your core values, you have a platform you can share with your guests and your team.

Core values also become a beacon to attract more people to your brand. Are you sustainability-focused? Does the ideology of farm to table move you? Are you family-focused?

Like does attract like. Your core values will draw people to you with similar values.

Step 2: Set the Standards

Human beings are great mimics. Maybe it's because our brain is wired that way to survive. In your restaurant, your team looks to you as an example. You set the tone every day by the actions you take. You get more respect and loyalty from your team by doing what you say you're going to do, when you're going to do it, and how you said you would do it. That's a little core value called, integrity.

Once you set the standards for your restaurant, it is your duty to lead by example. If you truly want to create a culture that exceeds ordinary, then you need to expect more from yourself than others do from you. You have to be the first to drink the Kool-Aid before your team drinks from the culture cocktail.

Be the leader they want to follow.

Step 3: Herding Cats

When you talk about the restaurant industry often, the word chaotic comes up. Just like herding cats, attempting to lead in a chaotic environment is futile.

The easiest way to lead your team is to hold them accountable for their actions. If you've set the standards and are being a prime example, then you gain permission to hold your people accountable, as well.

Clarify roles. **Talk to your team about your expectations.** Don't assume they get it.

If you can't measure it, you can't manage it.

If someone on the team strays too far from the standards and cannot deliver on the expectations, it's your responsibility to replace them. That's why it's so important to be constantly recruiting. You want a good bench of talent if you want to have lasting success in this industry. Great restaurants are always recruiting and adding top talent to their roster.

Step 4: Communicate Constantly and Consistently

When you're striving to build a successful culture, you cannot over-communicate. You need to be like Joel Osteen; captivating the crowd through creative storytelling. That's your job; to tell your brand story.

Problems arise when owners and operators talk about core values, standards, and expectations only at the beginning of the onboarding process. Without reinforcement or leading by example, three or four months down the road, they wonder why the employees change so much.

Without awareness of their culture and the process to build and reinforce it, is there any wonder they are surprised with excessive turnover?

Your communication with your team has to be three things: clear, consistent, and constant.

Clear - don't assume that your team understands what you're saying. Always ask if they need clarification and have them explain it back to you.

Consistent - your message has to be consistent from day-to-day and employee to employee. There can only be one standard, and you have to be the gatekeeper of that. Once you start having different standards for different people in different situations, you have embarked on a downward spiral that is hard to come back from.

Constant - repetition is the mother of all skills, and your team will need to be constantly reminded of your core values, standards, and expectations. It has to come from you and not from some cute poster you put up in the employee break area thinking it's going to reinforce your message. If you do, you are fooling yourself.

In the end, remember that your culture is your brand, and your brand is a reflection of your culture. The two have a symbiotic relationship and thrive on each other. Great culture creates iconic brands like Disney, Apple, Shake Shack, and Chick-fil-A. When you build your culture, you build your brand.

How far do you want to take yours? ***Good, great, or legendary?***

Foolish Pride

"No. It has to be my way, and I fucking want Martelli pasta!"

Ned, the executive chef, screamed at the Foodservice vendor on the phone. "You'll get it, or I'll buy from another company!"

Ned is a rising culinary talent. The owners of the restaurant where he is the chef ruling the kitchen with an iron hand brought me in to coach him. He thinks I'm hired to help him with systems and organization (which does come down the road). I'm there because he is tearing the team apart due to the one thing that kills many kitchens...*his ego.*

If you haven't heard of Martelli pasta and why he is obsessed with it here's why. Since 1926, the Martelli family has produced their artisan pasta in a medieval town in Tuscany. With simple techniques and traditional beliefs passed down from generation to generation, the Martelli family still manage the entire pasta production using 100% Italian, first-grade durum wheat to give birth to only five classic shapes. The wheat flour is manually worked into the dough using cold water. Then, it is extruded and cut with bronze dies and air-dried for 50 hours (compared to industrial pasta that is oven-dried for 30 minutes). This process gives the pasta a rough surface and special porousness, perfect for catching pasta sauce.

This restaurant is more of an upscale lounge food with a three-course menu for a dinner theater (think roaring twenties and *The Great Gatsby*). The show is a live burlesque production with three shows a night, and they seat around 125 people. It has nothing in common with haute cuisine like The French Laundry in Napa Valley run by celebrity chef Thomas Keller.

This place is more like an in-house catering set-up, and the chef can't get his head around it.

Highly creative chefs can find quick success due to the food they cook. Hey, when you can make food that dances across the palette, people tend to overlook those other skills that contribute to long term success like knowing how to not only make amazing food but making money at it too.

The restaurant is doing over $3M in sales and can't make a profit.

Ned is ordering steaks from Oregon that is FedEx delivered to the restaurant. He buys high end imported cheese to micro-plane over a signature eggplant Bolognese pasta dish.

The owners don't know what to do, so they contact me. The chef knows what the owners want; he has his vision and agenda for the food. Like many, he took the job with a hidden agenda that was not communicated.

Ned looks busy when you see him in the kitchen. *Being busy is not always a good thing.*

It's far better to be effective.

Ned sees the business as a vehicle to promote himself. He doesn't care about costs; he is more concerned about his image. His ego is writing checks that the owners are paying for, and they are tired of it. There is a lot of culinary talent out there that can make food that can come close to a religious experience; few can do that while building a team and make a profit.

The restaurant industry is saturated with talent that cannot run a P&L.

As competition gets more intense, owners are demanding that chefs have both culinary and business skills. With the right mindset, skills can be taught (if the person is teachable and coachable).

Getting through to Ned is the challenge.

Not all of this is on Ned, of course. The owners allowed the culture to grow into a monster that now is threatening to destroy the entire brand. Culture is a living thing. If it is not carefully cultivated, it can become tainted and turn toxic. Restaurants search for young talent and usually hire them based on one side of the coin; their creative skills.

A bad culture in a restaurant is like a virus that slowly infects everyone it comes in contact with. The root of all of this pain is improperly addressed expectations. The owners failed to communicate their expectations, and now it's a free for all. If you don't tell your team exactly what you want, don't get upset when they make things up on their own.

When I worked for Wolfgang Puck, there were very clear expectations that you were told from the beginning. They were non-negotiable, and if you crossed the line, you would know very quickly.

My work with Ned is slow. We take a few steps forward, and then he takes a few steps back. He can't get past the idea that the business exists to make a profit and is not a vehicle for his food. I can coach people only if they are open to new ideas and solutions (coachable) if they are stuck and resistant to change, it's a short trip as my client.

Contrary to some beliefs, coaching is not about changing people; it's about giving them the tools to change themselves. No one ever changes long-term for your reasons; they change because of their reasons.

After a couple of months, there are positive results with how Ned sees himself and his role in the restaurant.

It does not last.

Ned's friends and family constantly tell him how great he is and that feeds that beast called the ego. He is told he is underpaid and works too much for the money. This leads Ned down the path of entitlement.

He starts acting up between our video coaching calls and my visits to the restaurant. He wants more money. He forgets the lesson on vision, culture, and purpose. Before long, poor Ned is back to square one.

The ego can be self-sabotaging. Arrogance demands attention and allocates in the present. They don't think they need to improve.

Arrogance blinds people to the world around them.

- Without awareness, people cannot see a need to change.
- Without leadership, a team cannot thrive.
- Without humility, all the talent in the world is useless.

The Addiction to Average

The dream to open a restaurant is alive and well in America. The good news is; around 14,000 new restaurants opened in 2017. Real estate is booming, and if you look around your city, you'll see new construction sites popping up. If you have the money, you can easily open a restaurant.

The bad news is 50% will close their doors by year three of those that survive, most limp along.

"I think I'll start a restaurant to break even."

-Said no one ever

So how do restaurants get in this trap? What happens from when they open to the point they have to close the doors? It can be summed up in five words: *they become addicted to average.*

If you remember back in school, we were graded on the bell curve. The bell curve was created to provide a "fair" distribution of grades among students.

Ten years ago, you would not see some of the things that are commonplace today. The Bell Curve for restaurants has slid to where "good enough" has become the norm.

The addiction to being average has taken hold, and it's deadly.

When you are average, you are where the most competition is. You become a commodity, and in a commodity-driven market, your selling point is price. The problem is the restaurants try to outprice each other in this game until one is driven out of the market. It's an expensive game to play with your profits (if you see any at this level).

How do you escape the addiction to being average?

Be Original

It's not easy to stand out in a crowded market, yet many restaurants try each year because they think they can do it better than the restaurant down the street. Another chicken wing restaurant? Another pizza place?

You're going to have to do better than that if you want to stand out.

Wolfgang Puck took the personal pizza to a new level when he introduced gourmet toppings like duck sausage and cilantro on pizzas back in the 1980s. In 2017, it was common to see exotic ingredients on pizzas. Just like anything at first, you will be an innovator and soon others will try to copy you. You have to keep pushing and updating your brand to stay fresh and current with consumer needs.

Have you ever been to a restaurant that changed owners or managers and felt it was "different"? The menu was the same, yet things just felt off. That is the power of culture in your brand. Your brand's culture is your protection against those copycat restaurants.

Culture is a double-edged sword that can build up or tear down your brand.

Raise Your Standards First, Then Get Others to Raise Theirs

If there's one thing that is sure to help you break free from the average, it's to raise your standards. It's easy to say you'll raise your standards and not do anything about it. Most people do this. It's called talking a good game. Your words and your actions have to be congruent if you're going to be taken seriously as a leader.

Hypocrisy is a team killer.

It's easy to go around and bark at your staff to pay more attention to the details, to be on time, to not make mistakes, to be friendly to the guest. The question is, does your behavior, and do your actions reflect the same standards? If they are, congratulations. You are one of the few that hold themselves accountable first.

"Change starts with you. Be the change you want to see in your restaurant."

-Donald Burns

Raising your standards is easy in comparison to trying to get others to raise their standards. Remember, people only do things for their reasons, not yours. When you get frustrated with your team when they don't listen or follow directions, it is because they have not changed their standards.

Here's a classic example of how you get your team to raise their standards:

It's a busy Friday night, and as you're walking by the pass-through from the kitchen, you notice a couple of plates that maybe weren't 100% perfect. You could easily yell at the cooks about following the plate specs and not caring, or you could try something different.

You could pull the cook to the side and say something more along these lines:

"When you put that plate in the window did you pause and think whether or not you should have served it? If you did, then you know the right thing to do was to fix it. Every plate you put in the window is a reflection of you, not me. You have great skills. Just know that great skills and natural talent can take you to the top. It's your character that will keep you there.

I challenge you to raise your standards. Not for me. Not for the restaurant. I want you to do it for yourself. When I look at you, I see two cooks. The one you are now, and the one you have the potential to be. Step up and be the cook I know you can be."

Will everyone you have that talk with follow through and raise their standards?

Of course not.

However, if you can get a few people to buy in and raise their standards to a higher level than what they were before then you will have started creating a culture where average and mediocrity is not tolerated. You'll attract better quality staff and the low performing ones quietly go somewhere else where average is the norm.

Changing culture and breaking free from the addiction to average is not easy. However, it is a journey you must take.

Failure to do that dooms you to the no man's land of mediocrity and pain.

The 3 Types of Restaurant Owners

When you work with over 400 restaurants a year, it's easy to see emerging trends and patterns in the behavioral dynamics that make up what could be defined as restaurant owner DNA.

To better understand these three types of restaurant owners, first, we must look at two unique theories that while worlds apart are necessary for understanding the complex psyche that goes into someone who decides to open a restaurant.

Look at Darwin's Theory of Evolution. We know that things change and human beings have known that to survive, they must change and evolve as well or risk becoming extinct.

Restaurant owners also need to adapt to this philosophy.

Markets change. Sometimes rather quickly. More and more restaurants open every year, making competition tougher and market share smaller. Restaurant owners that fail to adapt quickly will get a first-hand experience of the natural selection process.

The second thing we need to look at is Maslow's Hierarchy of Needs. This is also called the theory of human motivation. A lot of business schools teach up-and-coming MBAs how to use this hierarchy or pyramid to understand the motivation of employees.

We adjust this a little to fit our restaurant model. The first level or base of the pyramid is the physical or material elements that compose a restaurant. Your logo, decor, tables, chairs, menu, staff, and food make up this foundation.

The next level would be sales. In Maslow's pyramid, it's called safety. A restaurant without sales pretty much is like a boat without a motor. Sales provide security, and when sales are down, it provides a ripple of uncertainty throughout the restaurant.

The third level would be social needs. We have a human need to connect and share our restaurant's story. This is where connecting on social media is so critical to the growth and evolution of the brand.

The fourth level gets into that area where many restaurants get into trouble... It's called publicity. At this level, all your hard work starts to bear fruit, and you start getting recognized for the brand you created.

This is also where a lot of restaurants make a bad turn.

You start getting a little positive attention from food bloggers, Yelp reviews, and maybe your picture in the local newspaper. While great on the surface, problems begin when restaurant owners start believing their own press. Their egos and pride become a roadblock to growth. Without growth, restaurants are very easy prey for Darwin's Theory of Natural Selection.

The fifth level in our Restaurant Hierarchy of Needs is the same as the one Maslow uses, self-actualization. Here restaurant owners have hit the Promised Land. The ego has been replaced with a desire for growth not only of themselves, but for the restaurant, the staff, and the community. Restaurant owners who can hit this nirvana of needs have a well-oiled machine... a team working with them building a very solid and profitable brand.

Maslow only had five levels to his hierarchy of needs. We are going to add a sixth level. This level is being borrowed from Stephen Covey's book, *The 7 Habits of Highly Effective People*. The 6th level we'll use is Covey's Habit #2: Begin with the end in mind.

We'll call it your exit strategy.

An exit strategy does not necessarily have to mean that your restaurant has to end. You could be building your brand to pass along to your children or family. You could be building your concept to franchise, or you could build up and sell it. As Kenny Rogers once sang, "Know when to hold em', know when to fold 'em.'"

Now let's look at our three kinds of restaurant owners, and you can see how far up our Restaurant Hierarchy of Needs they get.

1. THE ENTHUSIAST.

You thought it was a good idea based on the fact that you dine out a lot, think you could do a better job, or want to build a business around your great home cooking (like momma's meatballs). Most have never have worked in a restaurant. The rest have waited tables or cooked while in college...over ten years ago.

This owner usually can only survive through the first two levels of our pyramid. If they have adequate cash flow and are willing to learn, they might survive. It's a very rough road, and the school of hard knocks has very few graduates. Chances of survival go up dramatically if they elicit the help of a business coach or mentor. Most will never ask for help because they're too embarrassed to admit they got in over their head.

2. THE IDEALIST.

These people have a vision that they will not vary from no matter what, even if it is losing money. They would rather go down with the ship than be open to change. They do not ask if their concept is right for the market, nor do they care. They think they know what the customer wants. Driven by ego and pride, denial usually brings it all crashing down.

If this owner starts his restaurant with this attitude, with deep pockets and a bit of luck, they might be able to hold out for a few years. However, their chances for long-term survival are very narrow because they are just not open to change.

In the 1970s there were a 1000 Howard Johnson's restaurants. By 2005, there are only eight. A combination of no vision, no reinvestment of capital, aging restaurants, a stale menu, lack of marketing, and failure to change brought about the demise of a once-great brand. _That's natural selection in action!_

3. THE REALIST.

These owners look at the restaurant as an investment. They have a clear plan to build a brand and an exit strategy for getting out. These owners hire top talent and let them play to their strengths. They are constantly learning and improving their business!

Most people open restaurants to make a profit. These restaurant owners make it to the top of our pyramid. They seek out advice from coaches, consultants, and they mastermind with other like-minded successful entrepreneurs. These people are the Danny Meyers of our industry. These owners create concepts that challenge the status quo and build brands that create raving fans.

Which kind of restaurant owner are you?

TEAM

"Drama is great for movies, bad for restaurants."

Donald Burns, The Restaurant Coach™

Why Some Restaurant Teams Just Don't Work

You are working hard to build your team, and maybe things don't seem right. The team does not gel together. You read the blog posts and books. You feel like you are doing and saying the right things...so what happened?

The best intentions are nothing without the right execution.
Knowing what to do is very different than doing what you know.
"Awareness precedes choice and choice precedes change."

You have to be aware of the problem... the *real* problem. This involves looking into the abyss of yourself as the leader, and we all know from Nietzsche that *"if you gaze long enough into the abyss, the abyss will gaze back into you."* Be aware that when you go looking for answers, you might not like what you find. The truth will indeed set you free after it first pisses you off.

Team building can be complex because it involves bringing a group of people with different dynamics together for the mutual benefit of the restaurant. *That can be a challenge at times.*

Mixed Messages

Communication issues account for most restaurant issues. It's either lack of communication or miscommunication. Mixed messages are a covert form of sabotage within your restaurant. Let's say the owner of a restaurant wants the beer to be poured for the guest at the table. The other owner does not like that, so they tell some of the team that it's optional. When you send out mixed messages, you get mixed standards. That brings inconsistency which welcomes mediocrity. Once mediocrity sets up residence in your restaurant, you will need an eviction order to get it out!

Mixed messages also contribute to team turnover. The last thing your team wants to be is bounced back and forth about what the standards are. People want to work for professionals and not having a clear, consistent message tells them that you don't have your act together.

No Plan

If you were dropped off in the wilderness, how would you get back to civilization? You would pull out your map and compass and plot a course to get back to town. Your map and course become your plan, and your compass is your guide. Without them, you'd wander around aimlessly until they sent out a search and rescue team to find you (unless a wild animal already ate you).

Your market can be just like being dropped off in the middle of nowhere. Without a solid plan (your plan) and consistent action making adjustments (your compass) you'll wander day-to-day hoping that your business makes it. Once again, this does not instill confidence in the leader of the team. Even the bible mentioned that "Where there is no vision, the people perish."

You need a plan, and you need to share that plan with your team. Get them excited about your vision and how you will get there with their assistance. Most people like to feel a part of something bigger than themselves. Contribution is a basic human need that many feel calls to them.

Hidden Agendas

While we are social creatures, humans also tend to be focused on self-preservation. This is not to imply that your team is evil; it's just that survival is hard-wired into our DNA. Look at how we form cliques in the restaurant industry....FOH versus BOH. Day team versus the night crew. Your restaurant versus the one across the street. A human flaw is that we tend to need an adversary to fight against.

Teams don't work when we have hidden agendas. This could be an internal conflict in yourself or maybe within a team member. Honesty and transparency build teams. Without those two elements, your team will never develop trust, and that is the foundation of all great teams. You don't have to like all the people on your team. However, you must respect them and trust that they will do their job the best they can.

No Defined Roles

Now, this is fundamental, yet shocking to discover that a lot of restaurant staff do not know clearly what their job is or worse think their job is one thing and it's quite different than what ownership might have envisioned. Talk about having an identity crisis!

If you have not sat down with the people on your team to have a clear discussion about expectations and exactly what their job is as you see it, then you are missing a key to building a winning team. On military Special Operation Teams, everyone knows precisely what the role of everyone on the team is and who will take care of what as it occurs. They have to know. The cost is too great not to be prepared and to practice their roles. While people might not have life and death facing them as Special Operations Teams do, there still is a heavy cost to pay for restaurants that do not build an effective team…*they close.* Jobs lost, dreams crushed, and lives changed.

Team Chemistry

Understanding behavioral dynamics is key to a well-running machine. Some personalities work well together and some that are like oil and water. Knowing how to put together a team that can work together is like creating a delicate recipe. You need the right balance of ingredients to make it work.

There are four basic behavioral traits that everyone has with one usually being your primary driver. Understanding this will open the door to better team development when you understand how people are wired.

Dominance (take charge trait): these people are the stay-out-of-my way people. They are rooted in the present, and they love to make things happen. Their biggest strength is that they get results. They can be rough around the edges and are not much into small talk. Given too much power without proper guidance, they can become tyrants. When you need a project to get done, you get a high dominance person to lead the charge.

Extroverts (people trait): these are the big-picture thinkers. They love people and get energy from being around them. They can be extremely creative, and they like to talk about their ideas. These people are natural "salespeople." They make others feel very comfortable and are concerned about personal appearance. They are sometimes so caught up in the dream that follow through can be a weakness. If you need a host for the party, you get a high extrovert.

Pace (patience trait): these people are the team protectors. They like harmony and a peaceful work environment. "Why can't we all get along?" is their mantra. They hold the team together like social glue. They want harmony so badly that they will shut down when confronted and it'll be a challenge to get them to open back up. If you need someone to bring people together for a common goal, you get someone who is high pace.

Conformity (systems trait): these people love facts, data, and systems. Nothing makes these people happy like rules and spreadsheets! Now they can tend to be more analytical and not as people-friendly as extroverts and pace traits. They will ask for more information or statistics until they feel they have enough information, which can slow down the team as they wait until they get what they need. If you need someone with attention to detail that also loves numbers, then get a person with high conformity.

As you can see, building a great team is very much a balancing act. Too much of one trait and not enough of another and your team will be out of sync. In the end, teams are about people and having the right people on your team is the best thing you can do to pull together a winning team that will work together to help you build the restaurant you have envisioned.

This is all very similar to another factor of my Pararescue training: *team runs.*

Team Run

"Pick up the phone pole and put it on your shoulders!", Sergeant Jeffries barks out. Was he serious?

Yes, he was.

During the first phase of Pararescue training called Indoctrination (Indoc or the Selection Course), the instructors push you physically and mentally to your limits. Everything is a test. You quickly learn that how you do anything is how you do everything. You also learn that there are strengths and weaknesses in your team.

It's been about five weeks at the OLJ (or Operating Location J, the name for the Pararescue Training center at Lackland Air Force Base in San Antonio, Texas. The class has thinned out quite substantially. We started with around 83 men, and now there are only 14 of us.

Every day starts the same way:

- Wake
- The Dungeon (a space in the basement of the building that resembles a gym you would see in a Rocky movie. It's barren except for a few mats and pull up bars. It's dark, and the smell of testosterone permeates the air). Here you go through a series of calisthenics: 8 count bodybuilders, burpees, and flutter kicks. By the end of the session, you are completely soaked and you feel like you've lost 10 pounds in water weight.
- Shower
- Chow (and you shove it down as much as you can in the limited time you have)
- Run (anywhere from 3-10 miles)
- Class. You go through medical physiology and dive physics.
- Chow
- Pool Training (timed distance swim and then the fun stuff...water confidence)

- Class
- Chow
- Study
- Lights Out

I should mention that when you are a Pararescue Trainee, you never walk anywhere on base. **You fucking run.** Everyone alternates from one side to the other, so you're staggered. When the class is full, it is a challenge. Once the team thins out as people quit, you get kicked less by the guy in front of you.

The morning runs were always an adventure, depending on the instructor. Sergeant Pepin liked to take you on what was known as a jungle run. You would go off-trail, through streams, crawl through pipes, and basically whatever other obstacles he could get you to incur. His runs were also at a very fast pace. This for me particularly sucked because I was not a fast runner, however, get me in the pool and there I shined. On land, I could manage to maintain the 7-minute mile pace needed on runs to stay in class. In the pool, I was a shark. The only guy faster than me was my classmate Bill Peterson who was a collegiate competitive swimmer.

Sergeant Buonaugurio would take you on a distance run. You needed to get the guys who could run fast to dial it down and maintain a steady pace. The distance runs would include quite a few rounds of "last man up," where the last two guys in the team formation would sprint to the front of the team to establish the new lead. The distance run usually included a monster of a hill towards the end to push the team.

Then there was Sergeant Jefferies, who was pretty much a wild card. He would make you chase wild rabbits as a team. His favorite things were extreme team challenges like the telephone pole. If you have never felt the weight of one, let me assure you that thing is fucking heavy! I don't care how strong you are as an individual; you'll never get that thing up and moving unless you work as a team.

You see, getting it up on your shoulders is one challenge, getting it a couple of miles down the road is the other. The first time you do it, it is exhausting as you try to figure out (team problem challenge) how to get this thing off the ground. At first, everyone is lined up in formation like we normally fall into. *Funny how we get into routines, isn't it?* Once we got the telephone pole up we soon realized not everyone on the team was the same height and this brought about a new challenge. Now we had to put the damn thing down and line up tallest to shortest. Which brought about another challenge, admitting that the guy you think you are taller than is actually taller than you. Self-perception can be a real bitch!

After that challenge is conquered, moving it at first is not so bad. Small steps in a coordinated team effort do work. It's the distance that messes with you. Jefferies never tells you how far you have to go with that telephone pole, and that is where the mental game comes in.

When adversity hits, you have two options. Option A: You can let the weight of all of it come down on you and give in to it. Option B: you can break the big into doable objectives or "chunk it down." It's like the saying, could you eat an entire cow? Many say no. *Yes, you can, just one steak at a time.* If the steak is too big, cut into smaller bites.

A few guys on the team would grumble about how far were we going. That negative energy could have easily taken over and taken down the team. Luckily, most of us refocused the team on a smaller objective. "20 more steps and then we switch shoulders!" Breaking it down made it seem doable. "Yeah, we can make it 20 steps."

How many times have you looked at a problem and just felt overwhelmed by it? It happens even to me at times. Then I just cut it into smaller steaks (actionable steps). Now, look at your team and ask how you can pull them into a project to make it happen. When I give clients advice and actionable steps to take, they assume I want them to do it by themselves. Usually, after a day I'll ask, "How is it going?" and they almost always pause *(the longer the pause, the worse the situation)* and they say it's "**Going okay**." I ask if they have brought in other people on their team to help with the tasks. They didn't because they assumed I meant it was for them to do. Then I ask, *"Did I ever say to do it all yourself?"*

Nothing gets better in life until you take on the hard things. Sometimes you will need to enlist the strengths of everyone on your team. Just like moving that telephone pole, it was not going to happen with only one or two guys. It required the entire team, focused and working together to move it. There are some things in life that you will have to face alone. Most things in your restaurant can be done better by a team effort. A true leader plays to their strengths and incorporates the strengths of each person on the team to accomplish more. That is the basis of team synergy. Each element alone is great; together, they are unstoppable.

A restaurant is a team, and below is a guide on team dynamics, what works, and what doesn't.

A Straightforward Approach to Build a Better Restaurant Team

Great restaurants are built with great teams.

As more and more restaurants come into the market, it has become imperative to build a team that can help you reach your goals. Long-term success starts with having a solid plan for team acquisition and development.

Today, it's not enough to just put up a help wanted ad and then hope for the best. Hope is not a strategy you want to invest in. As competition gets tougher, you will need to become outstanding. That means you must stand out in your market.

Failure to do so will keep you stuck in the middle with the average. The last thing you want to be in a competitive market is average. Being average sucks.

Here are three straightforward ways you can build a better restaurant team.

Be a True Leader That Attracts True Talent

Look at the word manager. What is the first part of that word? **Manage**. A manager manages the day-to-day grind and never really gets ahead on tasks. These are the people who allow the restaurant to run *them*. They are always busy, but they are not very effective in building a team that can thrive.

Managers are in survival mode.

Now, look at the word leader. What is the first part of that word? **Lead**. That means exactly what it implies... you need to set the tone and the example. True leaders understand that to be a great leader is first to lead yourself. There are way too many people who call themselves a leader but live a hypocritical double life.

Being a leader is really about making sure you are at your best. That means taking care of yourself so you can be in the service of others. That means putting in the energy to develop your skills. That means learning and growing in your development so you can teach and train others. Think you are a leader? Then answer these questions:

1. *How many books have you read this month?*
2. *How many times have you worked out (gone for a walk or to the gym)?*
3. *Did you make your bed this morning?*

Wait. Make the bed? What does that have to do with being a leader? A lot. How you do anything is how you do everything. Making the bed shows commitment to a simple yet profound task. It starts the morning off with a completed task and sets your day up for more success.

Your team is looking for leadership. They crave it. They want it. It is your responsibility as a true leader to step up and deliver for them every day. True leadership is not a part-time job; it's every day.

When you develop yourself into a true leader, an amazing thing will begin to happen at your restaurant... you will start to attract talent. Like attracts like and when you become your best self, you will attract better talent to your team.

Now, if you are having an issue finding people to work for you, this might be a good time to hold up a mirror and ask yourself this question: "Are you a leader that is attracting or repelling talent?"

If you are honest, that might upset you. Good. Being upset is the first step to change. If you want to become a true leader, then you must first realize where you are now, no matter how bad it might appear, then make a plan and create a vision to determine how you want to be as a leader. Take action every day to close the gap from where you are to where you want to be.

Give Them Room to Grow

Everyone craves growth. It's human nature. We are wired to evolve. If you do not provide growth and learning opportunities for your team, they will seek them at another restaurant.

Too many restaurants only offer training when people first start. The typical 3-5 day training system is the average. Average training yields average results. We have to do better as an industry if we want to be attractive to younger generations that crave learning. This is not optional any longer. The restaurant industry must embrace, grow, and develop their people if they want to be competitive in the quest to hire and retain.

Some big corporations are known for their "perks." Restaurants would be wise to adopt this mindset in training and personal growth plans for everyone on their team. That is why online training platforms are ideal to invest in. Small, easy to digest training courses that will feed your team's need to learn.

You can also share articles you read on the Internet and books you have read as a leader (remember that leaders are readers). You will need to talk with your team and craft a personal development plan that keeps them on track for growth.

Growth is not just about getting a promotion; it's about growing in skills and growing as a person. Too many people think that if they do not have a higher position to promote someone into, then they do not provide growth. That is an inaccurate mindset that is holding you back from making growth and training plans for your team. It's just an excuse and excuses keep you trapped in the land of average.

Be Grateful and Thankful

There is nothing as powerful as these two simple words: thank you. It's true. People want connection and appreciation. At our core, we are social creatures. We come together to live in communities and cities due to this need.

Why do you think we visit restaurants? It's not just about food and beverage. If that was the case, people could easily drink and eat at home. We dine out because we want to be seen. We want to be recognized. We want social connectivity.

Your team wants that too. Your team wants to be appreciated. They want to be recognized for the good they do. Too many times, we focus in on the negative things people do and keep reminding them about them. Honestly, it's easy for humans to look for the negative because we are hardwired for it as a survival mechanism. It's called negativity bias, and it can get the best of a team if we do not look out for it. But when you focus on the dark side of things, that energy can spread quickly among your team.

As a true leader, you need always to be monitoring your energy and that of your team. When you see it going towards the dark side, you must step in and step up to revitalize that. The first step is to create a culture of appreciation and gratitude. That starts with you. You need to be an example.

Here's an easy way to start: at the end of every shift, walk up and personally thank everyone on your team. Make a sincere compliment and point out something they did that elevated the experience for the guest or helped the team. If you do this every day and are sincere, you will see a change in the energy of your restaurant. **You will also see a change in yourself.**

It's easy to build a better team when you start with a solid foundation. Step away from being just a manager and take a step towards being a true leader. Do you want to know the big difference between a manager and a leader?

A true leader uses these three words every day: I OWN THIS!

Finding the Right Chef for Your Concept

You found the perfect location. You have an idea for a concept. Everything seems to be coming together just as you envisioned. All you need now is some culinary talent to bring your dream to life. Finding the right chef for a new concept or replacing a chef for your established concept can be a challenge.

The problem is that in today's market, not all chefs are created equal. It'll take some research and some investigative skills to get the real scoop on if a potential chef is a culinary wizard or a culinary wannabe. Here are a few ways to make sure you get the very best for your business.

Check Social Media

Today the world is so connected by social media that you have a wealth of information available with just a few clicks. Start by googling their name. If they have been a chef for any time, they will have something show up. Search both by their name and also add the title "chef" to the search, especially if they have a pretty common name like John Smith.

If they have any press out there at all, they will appear in a google search along with photos of themselves.

Take a look at their other profiles as well on sites such as Facebook, Twitter, and Instagram. Here is where things can shed some light on the person they are, and you might see a few red flags pop up. That young chef with a profile picture of him squatting down in front of his car throwing some hand gestures that might offend a few people will tell you something about their character.

Those angry tweets about the government and racial slurs might get them a following on social media; however, having that kind of anger in your restaurant is not a smart move. Anger is anger, and eventually, it comes out either physically or verbally.

In either case, you have an undesirable outcome.

Instagram can give clues into what people find interesting. Check out what they have liked and what they post. Everyone has a "social media persona," so you need to check to see if it is compatible with your brand. Social media is so tightly connected today with a brand that you want to ensure that your future chef has a personal brand out there that works with your brand and not against it.

Call Real References

Anyone turning in a resume will give references. People will only write down people who give them a positive reference.

Dig deeper.

Skip the personal references. You want real work references for the places they have worked. Do not ask the standard boring reference questions like, *"Was Chef Smith dependable?"*

Let's try things like:

"What was the best dish they made? What was the worst?"
"Did they ever mention any chefs they admire?"
"What did they do to learn?"
"How are their skills in training?'
"Can you recall anything they did consistently for self-care?"
"How do they handle bad guest complaints?"
"If you had one last meal to eat, would you want them to be the chef?"

Questions like these are a little outside the norm, yet they will get you some great information. You are looking for patterns of behavior. Learning, pride, role models, confidence, emotional intelligence are traits you want to look for. There are a lot of chefs that can cook amazing food, yet are unable to keep it together emotionally. Self-control and self-discipline are the foundations of leadership, and your chef is the leader of the culinary team.

Check for Business Skills

As mentioned, there are a lot of chefs out there that can cook their ass off, very few that can lead a team and make money at their craft. Culinary talent without business sense is a real issue you want to be aware of. That is an Achilles heel that can cost you a lot of money.

Profit is not a dirty word.
Ask them to write a short menu for your concept. Make sure to give them plenty of details about your brand and then see what they develop. You want a chef that understands your brand and can create a menu that accents and does not take away from your identity.

Give them a test of their business acumen on financial controls. Give them a sample recipe and a sample spreadsheet of what the items cost and have them calculate the food cost for that recipe. Do this in the interview and watch their body language.

You may be shocked at the look on someone's face when they are asked to calculate food costs. However, if a chef is unaware of this, it is unlikely they can make money for you. It does not matter how great their food is if the restaurant fails financially.

Check Flavor Dynamics

You, of course, need to taste their food to see if they can truly back up their resume. This also is a great time to check out "how" they work. If you are an existing operation, pick a time when they can come in alone to take what I like to call is the "Johnny Cash Test."

In the movie, *Walk the Line,* Joaquin Phoenix portrays the famous singer and is auditioning for record producer, Sam Phillips. He starts with the standard gospel song and is quickly shot down. Phillips proposes a question to him, "If you were hit by a truck and you were lying out there in that gutter dying, and you had time to sing *one* song what would it be? One song that people would remember before you die. One song that would let God know how you felt about your time here on Earth. One song that would sum you up."

Ask your chef a similar question.

What one dish would you prepare that would make people remember you? Listen to how they describe it and the tone they use. Are they passionate about it?

Next, hang in the kitchen and have them make you a dish with what is commonly known as the "mystery basket test" as you see on the TV show Chopped. This is a great test to see "how" they work. There are a lot of clues to how they will perform by just watching how they organize a recipe and their technical skills. Are they pulling together their mise en place in an orderly fashion or just "winging" it? Are they using solid techniques? Do they work clean? Sloppy work produces sloppy results.

Ask questions while they are prepping and see how they react. Are they cool and calm, or do they seem irritated and nervous? Do they move with "economy of motion" (no wasted steps, very smooth and deliberate)? Remember that the chef sets the tone for the team. If they are running around like a chicken with their head cut off, how do you think the rest of the team is going to act?

Body language accounts for 55% or more of how we communicate and will allow you to see how this potential chef will perform under the pressure of service.

Final Thoughts

Finding the right chef can be a challenge. Panic hiring is never the answer. The chef position is a critical element to most restaurant brands, and the process needs to be respected.

How a chef handles the little things is how they will handle the big things.

A lot of chef's interview well. They know the right words to say. Then, they get in the kitchen, and you soon discover that they cannot control costs or seem to be able to lead a team. As they say, "all show and no go."

Attention to detail sadly lacks by a lot of wannabe chefs who want to do the creative stuff and not the business stuff. You need both elements to if you are going to find the right culinary professional for your concept. Like a well-balanced recipe, you need all the ingredients to come together to work in harmony.

Great chefs are multidimensional, and your brand cannot afford to settle for anything less.

No One is Reading Your Employee Handbook

You just hired that superstar. You are excited to get them started and on the team. You hand out your training materials and go over them. So far, so good. Or is it? You notice that after a few weeks, the new superstar you thought would become an asset has become like the rest.

What happened?

You didn't onboard them to buy into your culture. You handed out boring generic training manuals that did little to embed your core values and vision to the team. Now they, are like the rest...walking zombies.

Smart restaurant operators can take a lesson from those known for having a culture that flows with hospitality. It starts with how you and your training materials are delivered. If you feel like you are stuck on the treadmill of average, then take note of how to get off and into the fast track of employee engagement and retention.

Start with Your Why

You need to connect and be able to explain your core values and vision in a few paragraphs. Sounds easy-right? Try this exercise: describe your restaurant as a tweet. You have 140 characters, and that's it. This is a great way to see if you can get to the essence of your culture and your brand. If you want to get the most of this exercise, then dig deep. Don't go for the standard fluff or what is known as "corporate speak." You probably won't get it right on the first try. Every time you rework it, try to pull out a little bit more authenticity.

Your core values are the building blocks of your culture. They tell the world who you are and what you stand for. They become a beacon for the guests and the team you attract.

There is power in clarity. Knowing your core values is an exercise that most do only in a cerebral way. You know your values; you just have not put them down on paper and shared them. Sadly, most people do not mind read, so writing them down is a big deal. Once your core values are written down, make it a priority to declare it and share it.

Share it and share it often.

You cannot expect your team to buy into your core values if you only share with them once or twice. As the leader of your organization, you must stand on top of your soapbox every day and preach.

Preach the standards.

Preach the core values.

Ditch the Generic Templates

All kinds of training templates exist out on the Internet. Most of them are about as dry as an article out of the New England Journal of Medicine. Boring is never a way to instill motivation.

This is not to say that you cannot *start* with a template. Just eliminate a lot of the language and words used. If you have ever read through some standard employee handbooks, you'll see a common pattern in the writing that can be summed up in one word... Negative.

In writing, they talk about "tone." If you have studied any communications class, you will know that communication is broken down into three numbers:

7-38-55
7% of how we communicate is the words we choose.
38% is the tone we use.
55% is nonverbal.

Look at that middle number 38%. Remember that old saying, "it's not what you say; it's how you say it." This is especially true when it comes to your employee handbook. Tone can be joyful, humorous, serious, threatening, formal, informal, positive, or negative. Tone in writing really should reflect your voice and character. When writing training manuals, most people lean towards more serious tones.

"If you do this and not that, there will be consequences."

No one likes to be lectured. The more you respect them and speak to them in a positive, engaging manner, the more you will get back in return... even in print.

The tone of your training materials should be in congruency with your brand. If you are a hip, high-energy, food geek Emporium, then your training materials better reflect that. If you are a high-end, chef centric, destination restaurant, then the tone you need must convey the attention to detail and professionalism your brand emulates.

Drink the Kool-Aid

There's nothing more demoralizing to a new team member than when they see their leaders not following the same standards that are discussed in the training manuals. A standard becomes such in the mere fact that it is non-negotiable. That's why it's called the standard and not a flexible guideline.

As the leader of your restaurant you must (without a doubt) be the example for everything that is written in your employee handbook. If there is something in there that you do not feel that you can abide by, then take it out. It's much better to have integrity and do the things that are in your training manuals, then to be seen as having double standards.

Not following your guidelines and drinking the proverbial Kool-Aid yourself causes drama. *Drama is great for movies, bad for restaurants.* What is the easiest way to break free from the drama? Simple, don't contribute to it.

Hypocrisy kills teams and destroys dreams.

Training is a Commitment

You have to have 100% commitment to training your team consistently and constantly. Do you think that handing out an employee handbook when they first start, going over it for an hour, and never discussing principles in the handbook ever again builds a great restaurant? Yawn...

Great restaurant leaders spend most of their time training and developing their team. Living a mindset of constant and never-ending improvement wins the day. The Japanese call this Kaizen. It's not just a word; it's a philosophy of their culture. You can always improve. You can always be a little bit better. You only get better with more and more training.

Look at professional basketball players. Do you think they shoot a dozen free throws and think to themselves, "Well, I have that down... no need to shoot anymore."

Of course not. Every practice, they drill on the fundamentals to the point where it becomes automatic...even instinctual.

The problem with most restaurants is that we entice people in our door to join our team by selling them an illusion. Be the employee you want to hire. Train well after the standard training is expected to be done.

If your team's performance or energy slips, the real question is not, "What happened to them?" The real question you should be asking is, "What happened to me?"

Are You Getting the Most Out of Your Team?

We hear it all the time: *"Teamwork makes the dream work."* Good saying. Very positive. But often, it's not true. And the reason is simple.

Some people on your team don't want to do the work.

So, what is a restaurant owner or leader to do? Let's dig into some basic human needs psychology and find a few answers that can help you inspire those that work with you.

Motivating the Unmotivated

First, let's get something straight — you cannot motivate anyone except yourself. People do things for their reasons, not yours. A true leader inspires others with the congruency of their words and actions. They walk their talk.

To inspire others, you must first be inspired by yourself.

Now, you can say your team is "not motivated." That's an easy out. Blame them. A true leader would realize that they do not have an unmotivated team; they just have not done their duty as a leader to inspire them. Here are three ways to correct that:

1. BE THE LEADER THEY WANT

Fundamentally, people want someone to step up and be the leader. As social creatures, we look for direction and input. It's hardwired into our DNA for survival. We band together for the greater good of the species.

We all want to feel safe at work and to grow. The team needs to feel that their leader will protect the unity of the team dynamic. A true leader makes sure to treat all team members equally and honestly. Integrity is a cornerstone trait of outstanding leadership. When your words and your action are congruent, you will build a team around you that trusts you. Teams are built on trust.

Your team needs to feel that they have the opportunity for growth. Growth is not just monetary. It's the chance to learn and develop as an individual, as well. The human race has survived thousands of years due to our ability to adapt and grow. If you do not provide your team with a chance to grow, they will quickly become disengaged at work. When that happens, turnover is not far behind, or worse, they stay and become the walking dead of negativity that destroys any team morale there is.

The guest experience will suffer, and profits will slip.

2. UNDERSTAND WHAT DRIVES THEM

Have you ever sat down and talked to your team about what their goals and dreams are? True leaders sit down with their team regularly to have a conversation. But no platitudes.

A real conversation is one where you listen... actively.

Listen to what gets them excited. Is it music? A movie they saw? A book they recently read? Who do they follow on Twitter, Instagram, Tumblr? Any restaurants they like? What is their favorite food? When you actively listen, you can find out what matters to your team. Listen and take mental notes. When you talk to your team, use those topics that they are interested in to start conversations. That is how you build rapport with your team.

Take a sincere interest in your team if you want to lead effectively. People don't care how much you know until they know how much you care. Make a pact with yourself to get to know your team.

All of them.

3. CONNECT TO YOUR MISSION

Mission statements are a dime a dozen. Some restaurants hire consultants or branding experts to come up with this elaborate string of words that, while they sound fancy and use all the right adjectives, they lack one thing: soul. A mission statement is not just words on the wall that you cram down the throats of your team during orientation, and they say it back when asked like a parrot. A parrot can always say the words they are trained to repeat. But a parrot cannot understand what they are saying.

A mission statement that works is one that resonates from your soul.

Buried in there is the stuff that legendary restaurants are made of. Great leaders know this, and they must craft a mission statement from the heart, with soul, and purpose.

You do not build a restaurant. You build a team, and your team builds your restaurant.

Why Your Restaurant Management Needs a Tune-Up

Things move quickly in the restaurant industry. Faster and better seem to be the keys for a lot of up-and-coming concepts. Adaptability ranks right up there with consistency for top-performing brands. If you don't have your finger on the pulse of the consumer, you will quickly find yourself left behind. Improvements in technology and state-of-the-art equipment push our industry forward into the future.

What about management techniques?

If you read the current headlines, restaurant turnover is high, and the prospects to fill those openings are low. Is it because we cling to outdated management styles that our current workforce (Millennials) have a difficult time understanding or accepting? Times are changing. Let's look at how you can bring your management up to date.

A Brief History

Management, as we know it today, started with the rise of the Industrial Revolution (1860). Strangely, having a career as a manager did not exist until the 1930s. Before that time, people were known as "captains of industry." Professional managers realized they had a responsibility to three groups: employees, stockholders, and the public.

The 1950s and 60s brought about the implementation of systems. The psychology of management theory was introduced. In his book, *The Human Side of Enterprise*, social psychologist Douglas McGregor broke down management into two categories:

Theory X – where the controlling and authoritative manager believes most of his employees do not like to work and will only work under the threat of punishment.

Theory Y – where the democratic manager believes employees can be trusted and generally want to do a good job and improve their skill levels.

The 70s were characterized as a more contingency type approach to management. People were saying there's no one way to match, and it all depends on the circumstances. The 70s also saw the introduction of William Ouchi's, Theory Z. This was an attempt to merge American and Japanese management practices into a more consensual and participative management style.

The early 80s saw the introduction of total quality management (TQM), where the emphasis is on managing the entire organization, so it excels in all areas. TQM brought about the best-selling management book, In Search of Excellence by Thomas Peters and Robert Waterman, which remains a popular book today.

Things didn't take off as far as new management theories until 2000 when Jim Collins published a book titled *Good to Great*. Here, we were introduced to what has been known as the hedgehog concept. Managers focus on the simple core concepts that allow the company to focus on performance in a few areas rather than spread out over a lot of projects.

If you read through all of these, you can probably see the management techniques and theories from the 1960s that are still prevailing in today's restaurants. Today's workforce is unlike any that have come before. Whether a gen-Xer, baby boomer, Millennial, or Gen Z, they have their strengths and weaknesses, and can't be managed like it's business as usual. It's time to make a shift.

Out with the Old, In with the New

Old: Command and control – the manager drives success.

New: Engage and empower – success is driven by tapping into the natural strengths of the team and unleashing that power to improve the organization.

Old: Goals and objectives – the team is forced to comply with company standards.

New: Purpose and values – the team is motivated by being a part of something they believe is truly meaningful.

Old: Processes and systems – changes are driven by the implementation of new systems and checklists.

New: Culture and behaviors – sustainable change are driven by understanding and altering how the team thinks and behaves.

What's the underlying theme here?

Managers have to realize that people on their team are more than a line item on a profit and loss statement. Actions speak louder than words; talk is cheap. Sure, they're clichés, but your employees notice.

Management Change Starts with Mindset

Would you say your management style is more like a game of **chess or checkers**?

Managers who use a checkers' style tend to be reactionary. When something happens, they react to the situation. These people are the firefighters, who wait around for some drama to pop up and then spring into action. They tend to hang out in the office and bark orders at the team. These managers subscribe to Theory X.

Managers who use a chess style tend to be more strategic. They look at the strengths of each team member and plug them into the game where they would best help the restaurant. While this type of manager is actively involved, they trust their team and allow their natural strengths to shine. These managers are usually working alongside their team – coaching, training, and reinforcing the standards. These managers subscribe to a new theory, Theory C.

Theory C is where culture is the new commodity. They understand while a lot of restaurants in their market might be able to compete with similar standards on food and service, it's their culture that separates them.

A Restaurant Coach™ Tip:

Before you start thinking you need a new checklist or a new written Standard Operating Procedure (SOP) to get your team to behave the way you want; you need to ask yourself a few questions:

1. Will doing this new checklist or SOP get compliance or commitment from my team?
2. Does this new checklist or SOP explain the "why" behind the actions requested?
3. Do I have the right people on the team, and are they in the right positions that play to their natural strengths?
4. Do I know each team members' natural strengths?
5. Am I a leader or just the boss?

Mindset and behavioral patterns are what makes or breaks systems. Are you setting the example or just expecting the team to set the example you talk about?

Making the Mental Shift into Being a Leader

You got that promotion that has you on the side of leadership. You have the skills, and your hard work has paid off. You made it.

Not so fast.

The skills that got you to the top might still be there. The skills you need for exceptional leadership are quite different. You may be in for a bigger challenge than you realize. It's also the primary reason that most hourly employees promoted to a leadership role fail. They have a difficult time making the transition since very few are trained or mentored on how to be a leader.

The Battle Field Promotion

The most common way people in the restaurant industry are promoted is similar to what the military does. The manager or chef who is their supervisor gets terminated or quits and the next thing you know the owner turns to you and says, "Congratulations, you're the new GM/Chef/Bar Manager (insert the appropriate title)." They give you some keys and a few passwords, and off you go into battle.

The biggest issue with this type of promotion is an assumption. We assume the new person wanted to take over the vacant role. Assumptions are dangerous to your restaurant. Did we ever ask the person if they wanted the extra responsibility? Usually, they feel obligated to take the role, and the lure of more money makes it easy to say "yes."

A staggering 87% of managers wish they had received more management training when they first became a manager.

Talk about setting people up for failure! Most restaurants throw people into a leadership role without the skills they need to survive. It's like throwing a person into a den of lions with only a spoon to defend themselves. It should come as no shock why we find turnover in management so high.

Cross the Invisible Line

When you were promoted to leadership, there was a line you crossed. Not a physical line that you could see (that would be too easy), it was a mental line that took you from being "one of the gang" to now looking out for the brand. It's a shift in mindset that many have issues with.

The best thing you can ever do when you accept any position is to make a crystal clear declaration of commitment to perform the duties and embrace the core values that position requires.

Know the Difference Between Sympathy and Empathy

The main reason many have a hard time and cross back and forth is because of two words that are confused often in leadership: sympathy and empathy.

The biggest difference is the emotional depth they bring. When you were just one of the gang, you pretty much had an emotional bonding that occurred, and when things happened to others, you became sympathetic to their issues. By definition, sympathy is an affinity, association, or relationship between persons or things wherein whatever affects one similarly affects the other.

Empathy is defined as the imaginative projection of a subjective state into an object so that the object appears to be infused with it.

The key here is that sympathy deals with the relationship one has to the feeling, and empathy has to do with an experience one has to the situation.

When your deep emotions get involved in leadership decisions, you can do more damage to the team, then you think. Let's say you go from being the executive chef to becoming the general manager. The new chef has been working hard and asks you for a Saturday night off. You sympathize with the same emotions you had when you were the chef and how overworked you felt. You allow him the night off. Then a bartender comes and tells you they would like to have Saturday night off and you turn them down because you remember the days when you were a chef that the bartenders didn't work that hard (in your mind).

When you sympathize instead of empathizing, you keep jumping back and forth across that invisible line. That creates a sense of favoritism among your staff. Think of all the imaginary divides that exist in restaurants that are purely based on emotions: front of house vs. back of house, day staff vs. night staff — all imaginary lines we create.

How do you stop this? Communicate your commitment to being a leader. Tell your team what you expect and what they can expect from you. Detach from sympathy and employ empathy in decisions. Be fair. Be consistent. That means looking out for the welfare of the entire team, not just the people you like.

Invest in Yourself

With not much more than internet access and a public library card, you can get the knowledge needed to get your Ph.D. in leadership. So why do so many sit back and wait for their restaurant to train them?

Time?

Buzzz. Wrong! You have all the time you need. We all have the same 24 hours in a day. There is no such thing as "time" management; in reality, it is event management. If you are not investing in yourself, It's just not a priority.

Having new knowledge is great. However, you need to learn how to apply that raw power. Seek out a coach or a mentor.

You need to keep two things in mind when reaching out:

1. You will need to handle rejection. While there are mentors out there, you might have to search for the right one. Try to find one in your town where you can meet for coffee or lunch on you (hey they are donating their time and experience you should offer to buy coffee or lunch).
2. Have a plan and specific questions. If you've done some work on your own and have been reading and taking notes. You want to use your mentor's time the best, and that comes from the questions you'll have from your self-studies. If you sit down with a mentor and ask, "Teach me to be a leader." You will see the famous head shake of disbelief (otherwise known as SMH).

A mentor can help you transition into leadership much faster than going it on your own and learning by trial and error. A true mentor will give you some of their time; they won't allow you to waste their time if you haven't done the homework.

Earn Their Respect

However, you came into a leadership role; you must understand that there are two kinds of respect: given and earned. Just because you are in that new role, the team will not automatically give out the respect like it's candy on Halloween.

Here's a little test to see if you have someone's respect: ask them to do something that is totally outside their job duties. Ask a line cook to help with dishes. If you have total respect, then they won't hesitate. *Any pause at all, and you need to rethink how you are earning respect.*

So how do you go about earning respect? It's quite simple, work side-by-side with your team. No one earns respect faster than a leader who is willing to roll up their sleeves and get dirty. If you are a chef when was the last time you cooked on the line on a busy night and not just barked orders at the team from across the line in the expo window? If you are a general manager when was the last time you threw on an apron and showed your team the art of hospitality by taking a table?

Leaders lead the team by setting an example.

Bad Model of Leadership

The biggest mental challenge new leaders make is trying to find their leadership style. Contrary to popular opinion that "great leaders are born"; great leaders are developed and molded by experience.

The bad news: Most behavior and habits are learned.
The good news: You can learn it.

If you have poor examples from the past of what a leader is, then it's time to question those things that don't sit right with you. Look back on the managers you have had and make a list of the good, the bad, and ugly. Adapt and embrace the good. You have to consciously break yourself of the bad habits.

Your greatest challenge when moving into leadership is making the mental shift and deciding for yourself what kind of leader you want to be. Seek out positive role models. Make a conscious decision and commitment to become a better leader. Work next to your team to earn respect and above all, be honest with yourself if you truly want to be a leader. Leadership is not for everyone.

If you decide to embrace becoming a true leader, then go all in.

Does Your Team Know the Difference? Compliance vs. Commitment

While there are several descriptions and definitions of employee engagement, my feeling is that engagement is a reflection of how they spend their discretionary time and effort.

The difference between someone who's not engaged vs. someone who is is analogous to the distinction between compliance and commitment.

When someone is compliant, they obey – doing what's asked of them but no more.

Typically, they're doing just enough to keep their job. They are doing it for your reasons. Conversely, someone who's committed will spend time and effort outside of normal business hours thinking about work and solving problems, finding better ways to get the job done, seeking out new insights, and then acting on them. They do it for their reasons. *They have bought into your culture.*

What creates commitment?

1. **They need to *have* motivation.** In other words, they need to be at least somewhat self-motivated to start with. If a person isn't self-motivated about what they're doing (not the company or their boss, but the actual work itself), they need to find a job that has the kind of work they can be excited about. *Sometimes people are not a good match for the restaurant.*

2. **The engagement of the person they report to – their leader/boss.** A motivated, committed person will soon become unhappy if their boss is someone they don't **trust and respect**. Leaders can build or undermine trust in several ways. It's often a matter of **integrity**. I'm not talking about honesty (although being an honest person is essential), but rather about a leader doing what they say they will do,

and being the kind of person they say they are. *Mistrust grows when someone doesn't follow through on their commitments,* and trust grows when they do follow through. Mistrust grows when someone claims to embrace certain values but acts in a manner at odds with them (**a hypocrite**), and trust grows as people consistently act in alignment with the values they say matter to them. When it comes to respect, *a leader demonstrates they respect someone when they treat them with respect and listen to their ideas.*

3. **The culture of the organization.** An organization which claims certain core values but acts in ways which demonstrate that those values don't matter soon causes widespread disillusionment and disengagement (*once again hypocrisy, you talk a good game, yet do not prove it with day-to-day actions*). It's the leader professing the importance of certain values but acting in a manner at odds with those values (be on time, yet they never are). When a company tolerates bad behavior, it demonstrates a lack of integrity, which leads to a loss of trust and respect for the organization. *It takes only one bad apple to spoil the bunch.*

4. **The initiatives of the company.** An initiative *without reason or a "why"* is simply a goal, and goals by themselves are cold, unemotional targets, lacking any purpose other than to make the person who set the goal look good. If an initiative is to drive more loyalty sign-ups, there needs to be a "why" to go along with the goal. *People become engaged and committed when they believe in what they're doing and believe they are making a difference.*

Restaurants are filled with compliant people will get the job done, and the results will be acceptable *(which means average, and you know how I feel about being average!).* But if the goal is to exceed just average results (mediocrity) and achieve outstanding results, then a committed team is required. Start by ensuring that skilled people are being hired who are self-motivated and aligned with the organization's culture. Ensure that leaders at all levels improve their interpersonal skills (Emotional Intelligence is a great place to start). Take a good hard look at whether the organization is living up to *the core values it claims to embrace.* And be clear about your "why."

It may not be easy, but nothing great ever is.

Emotional Intelligence Exercise

Let's work on building *emotional intelligence*.

Write down the top 5 positive emotions you are in touch with the most:

1   .

2   .

3   .

4   .

5   .

Example: Passion, love, courage, ambition, creativity, focused, driven.

Now, write down the top 5negative emotions that are holding you back:

1   .

2   .

3   .

4   .

5   .

Example: fear, resentment, anxiety, reactive, hesitant, distraction, rude,

anger.

Why Your Staff Hates Your Manager

You go out of your way to recruit and hire a great manager. They have experience and excellent references. During the interview, they said the right things, were polite, well-groomed, they even looked you in the eye when they shook your hand.

They start, and you train them. Maybe not as much as you should have; however, you justify it by telling yourself, "they have experience, they'll be able to figure it out." You have visions of the team coming together, sales increasing, and profits flowing into your bank.

Two months later, things haven't seemed to become any better. Why?

1. THEIR SKILLS ARE NO BETTER THAN THE REST OF THE TEAM

In the restaurant world, actions do speak louder than words. If your new manager does not have superior skills to the people they supervise; strike one. It's hard to give respect to someone who can't do a task better than you.

2. THEY'RE HYPOCRITES.

They direct the staff to do things one way, and yet they are seen doing it a different way. Having a manager who cannot abide by their own directions or standards is a step down the path to team dissension.

3. THEY PLAY FAVORITES.

Most managers will say that they do not play favorites. The truth is, that most do. When you work long hard hours with others, it's easy to fall victim for what is known in Gestalt Psychology as the Law of Proximity. We tend to form tighter connections with those we are around more frequently.

4. THEY GOSSIP.

Most people enjoy gossip. The German's even have a word for how some people derive pleasure from the misfortune of others, it's called schadenfreude. Gossip mongers do nothing good for any team. Gossip tears teams apart.

5. THEY'RE NEGATIVE.

Negative managers are a rod in the wheel of team dynamics. Culture flows down, not up, and culture starts with the owners and management team. Seldom (if ever) do you see the attitude of the dishwasher have an impact on the culture of a restaurant.

Negative emotions are so addictive that our brains will seek out experiences and situations that evoke negative feelings.

The same area of the brain that seeks out pleasure also seeks pain. You may be wondering why this happens, well, it's really simple: Negative emotions activate both the beta-endorphins and dopamine pathways in our brains.

6. THEY'RE LAZY.

If you have a manager who hides in the office on the computer instead of working side-by-side with your team and engaging with your guests, then you have a lazy manager who is an expert at acting busy without getting results. They always have an excuse for why they can't get to that task or work with the team. When the team does ask for help, they'll give an excuse why they cannot. They want to be the boss of the team; they do not want to work as part of the team.

7. THEY'RE TERRIBLE COMMUNICATORS.

These managers look down on the team. They are self-absorbed and talk down to people instead of talking with people. Usually, they are quite clever and masters of illusion. You don't see them talk to your staff like that. They always seem nice in front of you when around the team. It's a Doctor Jekyll and Mr. Hyde persona that will create a high turnover of your top talent who will not tolerate this behavior.

8. THEY'RE A DRUNK/ADDICT.

Be careful of the manager who right from the start is constantly telling you that they don't drink. If they have not tamed those inner demons, they will come back when faced with a stress trigger that'll send them back to the dark side. Even with random drug testing and pre-employment testing, it hard to spot an addict who hides it well. Your team might see something as a red flag before you do, so pay attention.

9. THEY BLAME OTHERS.

You catch them doing something wrong, and they blame it on another team member. Being a manager is about becoming a leader. Leaders step up and take personal accountability for themselves, and they stand up for their team. Some managers will always be stuck as far as personal development and will never move towards being leaders.

Interview multiple times, ask out-of-the-box questions that can reveal their personality and depth of knowledge. When owners say that there are no good people to hire, perhaps they are not the kind of owner that attracts and retains top talent?

Sometimes the person who is holding your restaurant back from reaching its potential looks back at you in the mirror every morning.

Don't Lead a Horse to Water, Make it Thirsty

Don't take this the wrong way, but your training sucks.

Well actually, you could take it the wrong way and say, "Screw this, I'm out" and stop reading here. Or you could say that perhaps this guy might be onto something and you should hear him out.

Still here?

Good. Let's dig in!

Training is often considered a part-time (or worse) a one-time job that is done when a new employee joins the team. We spend a few hours and days with this new team member expecting them to be the bearers of the standards. Then we end up firing them for not doing what we had explained during that brief window of training. Most restaurant training programs (if you can even call them that) are just setting people up for failure. Then we sit back and throw out some shade like, "there are no good people out there," "they weren't a good fit for our restaurant," "kids today just don't want to work," or my favorite..."If I want anything done right, I have to do it myself."

Yeah, your training sucks.

Big time.

So, what is a leader to do? First, is to admit that you don't have a training problem, you have a culture problem. That culture problem changes when you step up to be the leader they desire and deserve! You're not going to like this next line: that starts with changing yourself. I know, it would be so much easier if everyone else around us would change.

However, when you consider for a moment how hard it is just to change yourself and you'll finally see what little chance you have of changing other people. The odds are not in your favor. If changing another person is not an option, what is?

Change the Culture

Here is one thing you do have control over as a leader, and that is the culture of your restaurant. Unlike the personality of people, your culture is a little more fluid like a river, and it adapts to what feeds it just like a river. A river can be just a trickle, and when heavy rains come down, it can turn into a raging powerhouse. Water in a river is energy. It's energy that drives your culture. That's on you.

So, what are you doing to set the example and become a better leader?

- *Are you taking care of yourself?*
- *Reading new books, blogs, or listening to audiobooks?*
- *Are you taking an online course?*
- *Got a mentor or coach?*
- *Are you eating better?*
- *Are you getting that anger issue under control?*

Change yourself, and your culture will immediately start to shift. Will it be as fast as you like? No. However, most things don't change as fast as we like. That's just how life is. If your culture has been out of control for some time, it's going to take about half of that time to get it back on track! So, if your culture has been like the Wild West for the last year, expect to put in a consistent six months getting it right. Sorry, that's just how it goes. You let your culture and restaurant get away from you so now it's time to strap in for the road to recovery.

PURGE THE VAMPIRES

You know they are out there in your restaurant. Those negative energy vampires that prey of positive energy and stuck the life out of it. Those that use sarcasm and little snide comments as weapons to bring down the energy level. Some might be your key people too. The really scary thing is that some might even be your family or friends.

These people are just pessimists who don't want to see the world as a better place. They want just to see it limp along and enjoy the misery. It's like a perpetual dark cloud follows them around all day. They want to bring those around them down to there level. It's time you stopped tolerating them in your restaurant.

I recently had a client who had a **NEV** (Negative Energy Vampire) that was his chef! As talented as the guy was, he was a Black Plague upon the morale and energy of the kitchen. That spilled over to the other members of the service team, and they became afraid to go back into the kitchen to ask a question or relay a special request from guests. Fear destroys teams, and it is death to your culture.

Was the owner excited about getting rid of his chef who had been with him over a year and helped open the concept? Oh, hell no. The conversation turned with one statement I told him,

"You can't control your restaurant until you control your culture."

The lightbulb clicked, and he finally knew what he had to do if he ever wanted his restaurant to thrive and not survive...eliminate the NEV's from your culture. Was he scared? **Yes.** Was he worried about not finding another chef that was talented? **Yes.** Did he take action in spite of fear? **Yes.**

Here is the interesting thing about fear. It never seems to turn out as bad as we thought it would. The client did find a new chef within days. With a better selection system in place, he upgraded his culinary talent big time. He hired a chef that shared similar core values and had the optimistic attitude required to excel at the job. Things in the kitchen have already turned around. The service team is being trained more about the food, and the guest experience scores are rising more each week.

Be Hungry

Cultures that foster an environment for learning always outperform those that train occasionally. Here's where culture starts to grow exponentially. When people are hungry to learn and grow. Too many look at training as a necessary evil. I have to give them the same standard 2-7-day training program, and then I'll throw them into a station or section where they either sink or swim. That is not a training system. That's a failed system.

Giving people the minimum training or education to do their job is why the system is broken. You set them up to fail and wonder why they didn't work out. It's because you didn't train them to **excel** at their job. You gave them a few key points (maybe a training manual), had them follow around a "trainer," and then cut them loose on your hard-earned guests.

The word training should be replaced with the word education. We need to develop our teams to where they feel we have a vested interest in their personal growth. This means that you, as the primary energy source for the culture, must be committed to learning as well. Why? Because that hypocritical attitude of "do as I say and not as I do" bullshit doesn't work with today's workforce. Yeah, you're going to need to up your game as a leader who sets the example if you want to attract and retain staff today. Leadership, by example, is the only way.

Share books, magazines, blog posts, and audiobooks with your team. Let them see you want to become a better leader by the way you are obsessed with learning. You see, you don't want to lead a horse to water; you want to make it thirsty. You don't train your team; you get them thirsty for knowledge. Once to shift from a training culture to a learning culture, you see some spectacular benefits:

- Reduced turnover
- Fewer staff calling in
- Increased energy
- Better guest reviews
- Fewer mistakes
- Increased profits

Culture is a foundational element to any successful brand. Culture is created by either default or design. You always want a say in the development of your culture. That all starts with becoming a better person and a better leader. Culture flows down, not up, and culture starts with you.

TIME

"Until you value yourself, you won't value your time. Until you value your time, you will not do anything with it."

- M. Scott Peck

6 Time Management Strategies for Restaurateurs That Actually Work

Imagine you look at your watch at midnight. At that one moment in time, you have exactly *1440 minutes* until you reach midnight again.

One thousand four hundred forty minutes – that's it. You can't borrow or buy more time.

Time is one of the most valuable resources we have. Most restaurant managers fail to utilize time to their capacity. Let's get this straight: you either learn to master time, or time will master you. This is why you need effective time management strategies.

If you Google up the words "time management," you will get 93,800,000 results. It seems like a lot of people are looking for solutions to manage their time better and want to get shit done.

So *why* is it so difficult to follow time management strategies? A lot of it has to do with our perception of time management. So here is a breakdown of a few of the barriers holding us back.

Truth: Most Time Management Strategies Don't Work

This is especially true in the restaurant business for one simple reason: most time management strategies were designed for those who work in 9 to 5 office jobs. Very few restaurants follow the normal grind of business life. Depending on your concept, your hours are quite a stretch from the normal cubicle worker.

Traditional to-do lists are the *worst* thing you can use. Most do nothing to further a project along. They are simply reminders of all the things we intend to do (that most of the time stay on our to-do list).

What baffles me is a lot of people take pride in the length of their to-do list. It's almost like a badge of honor to have a long list to show people how busy you are. The real question is: are you *busy*, or are you *effective*?

Let's take a look at six steps that can help you bend time like a Jedi Master.

1. DITCH THE "I'M BUSY" STORY

You're busy. I'm busy. Most people are busy.

We tend to be that way because life, at times, seems like a spectator sport. Throw in the fast-paced nature of the restaurant industry and things tend to move even more rapidly. However, this should not deter you from adopting or abiding by time management strategies.

2. DROP THE "I DON'T HAVE TIME" MENTALITY

This one is almost as damaging as throwing around the "I'm busy" story.

Let's be clear on the concept of time ownership. You never really *own* time. You use time. People who use the excuse of not having enough time don't have their priorities straight. How could people like Steve Jobs, Elon Musk & Danny Meyers accomplish so much given that *they have the same 1440 minutes each day?*

They prioritize their tasks with what is most important to them and the brand, and then they take action. A lot of action.

3. BREAK IT DOWN

Traditional to-do lists are nothing more than a collection of good intentions. These to-do lists should never define your time management strategy.

However, you can use your list to your advantage if you understand how to chunk or group things into categories. This is an effective way to organize your list. You could use locations or even the name of a person you interact with a lot. Categories could be kitchen, bar, office, service team, culinary team, managers, and vendors. Now when something pops up in your mind, just put it under the appropriate category.

4. THE POWER OF THREE

When you make your list, you will probably see a couple to-do's that stand out and know they need your attention.

Pick out three. Just three.

Humans tend to overestimate what we can do in a day and underestimate how long it takes to do a particular task. You think you can knock off a dozen items on your to-do list today, yet when you sit down to do a task (like writing a blog post on restaurant management strategies), you find that time just got away from you.

Don't feel bad. It's human nature.

Three is a beautiful number because it's manageable. It's also memorable. How about the Three Musketeers or the Three Stooges? How many ships did Columbus bring to the New World? *Three*. In China, three is a lucky number, partly because it sounds a lot like the word in Chinese that means life.

Stick with three.

5. MANAGE YOUR CALENDAR

When you think about something, it's a dream.
When you start talking about it, it becomes a possibility.
When you put on your calendar, it's a commitment.

If you truly want to master time, become a black belt in getting the things done that you have on your calendar. People who get a lot done schedule *every-thing* on their calendar and use it as a compass throughout the day.

They also take advantage of focus blocks. These are short blocks of time that you place in your calendar where you are focused on the task at hand: no cell phone, no email, no Facebook. Focus blocks are generally more effective in 20 to 30-minute increments. You won't need a lot of time to make progress on a task to move it forward, but you will need focus.

You hear people say that time is money. It's not – *money is money* – but the real currency in today's world is focus. That's the real secret of time management. Controlling your focus for short periods is the key to success.

6. SET YOURSELF UP FOR TOMORROW

Peter Drucker once said, *"If you want to predict the future, create it."*

If you want to master time management strategies, you have to plan for them. The best time to do this is not on your way to work in the morning, but instead the night before.

After services die down, you probably find a little solitude in the calmness of the restaurant. This is the perfect time to put your focus on those three things you want to tackle tomorrow. Look at the categories on your list, pick up your three, think about what action you have to take to move one task forward, and make a commitment by scheduling time on your calendar.

"If you want to predict the future, create it."

– Peter Drucker

Restaurants are far from "predictable." Every day brings along a little excitement or adventure. The best way to get your three things done is to schedule two focus blocks first thing in the morning. That way, you can designate sometime in the day for yourself before the demands of others (i.e., the staff, the vendors, the guests) start to demand your focus and attention.

Restaurant Time Management Strategies

Focus is your power. You can't control time. The only thing you can control is your focus and energy. Where focus goes, energy flows. Tap into that, and you'll see your productivity powers grow stronger than you could ever imagine.

7 Bonus Time Management Hacks to Get More from the Day

The world keeps moving faster, and we must move along with it. So as the world gets more connected, our lives get more complex, and yet we all seem to run out of hours in the day to get all we want to be accomplished. Let's face the facts that most people are terrible at spending their time wisely. In the world of business coaching, the topic of time management is almost always on the agenda. Even those who are defined as being "successful" are looking for ways to streamline tasks to bend time to their will.

The only real lesson to time management is to understand this basic concept: You never manage time, you manage yourself. Here are seven down and dirty time management hacks to get more done in 24 hours.

1. SET YOUR FIRST MEETING OF THE DAY WITH YOURSELF!

The best way to set yourself up for success is to make sure you are investing in your number one resource...yourself. Starting the day out fully charged is insurance to get the most out of any day.

Just like you would not skip an important business meeting, you need to schedule a morning meeting with yourself; for yourself. Have a morning "hour of power" to get your mind and body in sync. You can go to the gym, go for a walk, do yoga or martial arts. The main thing is that you need to move your body to get the blood going. The restaurant industry is notorious for burnout and unhealthy lifestyles. You work long hours (mostly on your feet), and we get little time to exercise. If you want a long career in this business, then self-care has to become a primary need. Notice the word need, not want. You will do whatever you have to do to get your needs met. If it's a want, it'll only happen if all the elements come together.

2. PICK 3.

Life balance is a myth. That might be hard to swallow since most of our lives; we are told that to be ultra-successful, we need to find the elusive balance between personal & professional.

It's not going to happen.

If the world was perfect, and there were no outside demands on your time and focus, then you might be able to achieve life balance. Since we know the restaurant world is not rose-colored and rainbows, let's focus in on what works. Pick only 3 top projects or things you need to accomplish in any given day. You can easily fill up a "to do" list and try to make it through that daunting task of trying to get it all done. If you pick only three things for the day, your chances of getting them done greatly increases.

So, start the day with your hour of power" or self-care meeting to make sure you are fully charged up for the day. Then look at your Big 3. Take immediate action on getting one of those projects moving. The key here is that the demands of others will come for your focus and time. Dedicate time to make sure that your agenda is getting the energy and focus it deserves.

3. LEARN TO SAY "NO."

People who work in the restaurant industry tend to be people-oriented (which is a good thing). We also tend to try to please everyone (which can become a bad thing). You will need to learn to say "no" gracefully to things that do not serve you. Time is the most precious commodity we have. You cannot get more of it, and once it's gone, that's it.

Now some things get put on your plate from outside sources that you may not have an option to decline. However, some things are totally within your control — watching TV, playing video games, surfing the internet, and other things that pull your focus away from what is important to you. The best question to ask yourself if you want a better life is this, "Is this (insert task or activity) going to move my life forward towards my goals and dreams?".

The quality of life you have is in direct proportion to the quality of questions you ask yourself. It's quite easy...if you want a better life, ask yourself better questions.

4. HAVE A PLAN.

Having a written plan is still the best way to stay on track and focused. You can use the old school method of pen and paper or use technology to get a handle on what you need to focus on. We're going to take a concept from David Allen's Getting Things Done Methodology to help clear our heads from the minutia that consumes most of our cognitive processing. When something pops in your head to do, you need to get it into a safe place to process later. The note app on your smartphone is perfect for this. Get it out of your head, or else it will begin to form a "mental loop." The issue with loops is that they tend to bounce around in our heads until they get solved.

Having a place to park all these random thoughts that pop up in your head is important (neuroscientists claim we have around 60,000 random thoughts going through our brain a day). This is a great way to get them in a place where you can go through them and sort them into action, reference, or delete them.

5. IF YOU CAN...DELEGATE.

This one ties into learning to say "no." So many restaurant managers do tasks that others could easily take care of. Things like scheduling, recording invoices, receiving orders from vendors are all tasks that can be trained. Here is the bonus, when you train your team to take on more responsibility they have a chance to learn and grow. That is a winning element to team retention.

If you give the excuse that you have to do everything yourself, then you have either one of these two issues:

A. You are obsessed with control and perfectionism. While striving for excellence and consistency is a common thread among great restaurants, it's very hard ever to be perfect.

B. You do not trust your team. If you do not trust your team, then you need to get a team you can trust. This might lead you to look at option A once more.

6. FOCUS MORE ON RESULTS THAN TASKS.

Focus is the only things you ever really can control. What you focus on and put energy towards gets done. The question to ask yourself is, "Are you focused on things that have an impact?"

While most restaurant owners and managers are always "busy." They tend to be focused on things that have little impact on improving the restaurant.

They focus on the price of their food from a vendor and spend a lot of time "shopping" pricing from multiple purveyors when they have never actually figured out the food cost of every item on their menu.

Most people become very **efficient** in their job duties. They are usually not incredibly **effective** in those jobs. Focus on the things that have a bigger impact on your business. If you have trouble figuring out the "right things" to focus on, then consider getting a business coach to help you.

7. MANAGE YOUR ENERGY, NOT TIME.

Here is the best time management hack of all! Time is just a construct of the mind. You cannot change time or manipulate it. It is an uncontrollable variable that most people seem to be either chasing or a slave to. To break free from that, you need to look at your natural energy patterns, and when you are in the peak energy "zone" use that energy to get the right things done.

Our bodies have a natural circadian rhythm (chronobiology studies the effect of how our bodies and minds work during the day). If you tap into this rhythm, it can give you the ability to get some shit done. Most people find that the mornings are best for cognitive thought, analytical thinking, or problem-solving. Afternoons are great for physical demands. The evenings tend to be a better time for creative processing.

Keeping your energy levels at peak states requires a commitment to exercise, drinking plenty of water, and making sure you are eating properly. These three basic elements provide the fuel your brain needs to handle all the variety of tasks that come at you during the day. We all know what happens when you run out of fuel in your car. Your natural energy levels are the fuel you need to get things done.

The restaurant industry can be very demanding. Taking time for self-care and giving yourself the gift of refueling your energy levels is just making sure that you have enough to give to others. In the end, you get back what you put your focus and energy into. Use it wisely.

Are You Busy?

If you consistently feel the counterproductive need to stay busy and to be doing a lot of things, write these words on a Post-It Note and read it every day:

Being busy is a form of laziness. It's lazy thinking and indiscriminate action.

Being busy is most often used as a guide for avoiding the few critically important but uncomfortable actions you must do.

Stop being busy and start being effective.

MENU

"My mother's menu consisted of two choices: Take it or leave it."

- Buddy Hackett

Telluride

In 1995 I did a consulting job up in Telluride, Colorado. It was one of my first. The sleepy little town is a step back in time to the Wild West. On my first day in town, I discovered the Mahr Building. It was the site of the original San Miguel Valley Bank in Telluride, the same bank that Butch Cassidy and three others robbed on June 24, 1889. The old bank burned and was replaced by the current building in 1892. It was the first of many banks that the famous outlaw robbed. I have always found history and the stories embedded in a culture fascinating.

I was hired to revamp the menu at a local restaurant that had been there since 1973. The owner at the time was a man by the name of Howie Stern (no, not the famous radio shock jock). I came in with the idea to shake up that town with my version of contemporary southwestern cuisine after a few years working as a chef in Santa Fe & Taos.

I worked like a chef possessed coming up with all these creative and innovative menu ideas. Once I drafted out the menu, I gave it to Howie to review. He sat there, silently reading my work. ***He didn't say one damn word.*** Finally, he looks up at me and says, "Take a ride with me."

We drove down Main Street, and he said, "See that big house on the side of the hill?" It was a beautiful mansion about 300 yards up the side of what was more like a mountain instead of a hill. "Oh, yes, stunning," I replied.

Howie asked me, "How much do you think a house like that costs?"

Me: "A million?" (I was guessing)

Howie: "A little over 3 million." Then he added, "Do you know who that house belongs to?"

I thought it had to be some celebrity, but I played it safe and replied, "No."

Howie said calmly: " That's my house. Do you know how I paid for that house?"

Okay, saying money would have been a smart-ass answer, so I went with, "No."

Howie: "*I sell a lot of fucking hamburgers! Don't come in with your big ideas. I want my menu to be improved, not a new concept for this town!*"

Point taken.

We upgraded the beef to include some ground brisket, and I developed some cool toppings like port glazed mushrooms, wasabi mayo and a jalapeño-bacon jam that became big hits on his already popular burgers. It was a hit.

What did I learn? That you must do market research before you start writing menus, and if you have a great fucking niche, then dominate it! Changing shit to change is stupid. Oh, and for those chefs out there. Your ego won't pay the bills or get you a house on the side of a mountain in Telluride. ***Drop it.***

Jedi Mind Tricks for Your Menu

Of all the things that can have an impact on your bottom line, your menu is your primary tool. Unlike retail businesses where people may browse and leave, there is a very high chance at restaurants that visitors will purchase something to eat or drink. Menus are more than just a list of items for sale, then. Your menu is a tool of influence and persuasion when designed properly.

The common mistake most restaurant owners make when it comes to design is they try too hard. Their menu becomes a dissertation of filler words and descriptions that leave the guest confused and overwhelmed by the number of words that fill up the menu page. The key is to understand that when it comes to menus, we don't read them, we scan them. If you want to have a more effective menu that really can drive sales, then you need to set up and design your menu for the way most people look at it.

While an entire book could be written on the psychology of menu design and menu engineering, let's focus on three simple Jedi mind tricks you can utilize to guide people to where you want them to buy.

1. ANCHORING

Back in the 1980s, psychologists discovered that exposure to certain words could encourage consumers to buy items they suggested. This is done through price comparison, and it works quite effectively.

Have you ever been to a high-end steakhouse and seen this on the menu?

PB& J + Louis Roederer Cristal
Handcrafted peanut butter & jelly + vintage sparkling champagne   197.00

Chilled Mixed Seafood Platter
mango butter lobster + chipotle shrimp + blue point oysters with green apple -black pepper mignonette 87.00

The restaurant sells very few peanut butter and jelly sandwiches with a bottle of champagne; however, they sell quite a few of the chilled mixed seafood platters. Anchoring works when you put the most expensive item first. After that, the item in place after the most expensive appears to be a much better value.

2. THE ONE POINT FONT CHANGE

Here's another easy one that uses how our brains are naturally wired to focus on a menu item we want to increase sales on. The oldest part of our brain is commonly referred to as the reptilian brain. This part of your brain is responsible for a lot of your survival mechanisms like the fight or flight response. It's hardwired to notice things out of the normal, such as, "Is that a saber tooth tiger about to eat me?"

Just as our brains can play tricks on us, we can play tricks to draw the eye to exactly where we want on the menu. Take a look at these items:

FROM THE GRILL…STEAKS & MORE!

24 oz. buffalo ribeye
roasted garlic mashed + baby carrots + merlot reduction 42

the ribeye
16 oz. center-cut steak + achiote potatoes + haricot vert + red wine butter sauce 35

roasted poblano & veal meatloaf
mashed potatoes + sautéed mushrooms + cabernet demi + red chile onion rings 20

brown sugar cured beef tenderloin
*our signature steak! 8 oz. hand-cut filet + wild mushroom
enchiladas + fire-roasted corn & pepper demi 28*

pine nut crusted pork chop
*12 oz. cut bone-in + roasted potato-vegetable mélange
+ red chile cream + parsnip chips 24*

bourbon roasted chicken
potato-parsnip puree + baby carrots + natural jus 22

Does any item stand out? The text size for most entrées in this example is 13 points. This restaurant's number one seller is the brown sugar cured beef tenderloin. There, the text size is 14 points. **A one-point font change causes the brain to take a second look.** That second look gives the entrée another impression in the brain, and many times, that's all it takes.

3. THE BOLD WORD

Remembering menu psychology, such as the fact that the brain scans menus rather than truly reading them, you can assist and guide your guests by using a simple technique to draw focus to keywords.

Take a look at the following menu items:

Kobe beef sliders
green chile +cheddar cheese + chipotle ketchup 9

lobster wontons
butter-poached lobster + poblano cream cheese + sweet chili dipping sauce 12

cornmeal-dusted calamari
tomato-basil sauce + lemon zest aioli 11

baked brie
roasted garlic cloves + apricot-green chile chutney + melba sauce 10

Now look at them again:

Kobe beef sliders
green chile +cheddar cheese + chipotle ketchup 9

lobster wontons
butter-poached lobster + poblano cream cheese + sweet chili dipping sauce 12

cornmeal-dusted **calamari**
tomato-basil sauce + lemon zest aioli 11

baked **brie**
roasted garlic cloves + apricot-green chile chutney + melba sauce 10

The eyes focus on the words you want the guest to find easily. Make your menu easy for the guest to find what they're looking for, and they will buy. Another cool technique is to take out the comma (,) between ingredients and instead use the plus sign (+). Most of us have been conditioned to know that the + means addition. So, in the case of the lobster wontons, the brain reads lobster wontons: I get butter-poached lobster **plus** poblano cream cheese **plus** sweet chili dipping sauce **for only** $12, that's a deal!

These Jedi menu tricks work best when it is a very clean and easy to read font (Sans Serif works very well). Stay away from cursive or funky fonts that make it difficult for the guest to read. The bottom line is to design your menu to make it easy for the guest to comprehend and see even in the romantic lighting of your dining room at 8 PM.

All menus are great when we're looking at them under the bright lights of an office. The true test is to take the menu into your dining room and take a look at it under real-world circumstances and see if it's just as easy to read. You might be shocked at the difference, especially when you can track menu items' profitability with menu software.

IS YOUR MENU TOO AGGRESSIVE FOR YOUR MARKET?

Take out your menu and look at it. Take it all in. How do you feel about your menu? Are you happy with it?

Are your guests happy with it?

Menu creation is easy. Anyone can pick out some items, put them on a menu, and try to sell them. The true art comes when you try to make a profit from that. Sometimes that is not as easy as some believe it is.

The answers are in the questions you ask yourself about your menu. If you want better results, ask better questions. The truth is liberating; however, at first, you'll be more pissed off. It's okay; emotions get people motivated. You need to trust the process.

So, let's get a little uncomfortable. Here are some questions you need to ask yourself while you have your menu in front of you.

Square Peg, Round Hole

Does your menu match your brand? This might seem like a simple question on the surface. You say you are a modern Southwest grill concept, yet your menu is mostly pasta dishes with only two grilled items. Are you a grill?

Your sign says you are a Mexican restaurant, yet your menu offers pizza. No, not pizzas inspired with roasted poblano peppers and chorizo, just plain pepperoni and cheese. Confused?

So are your guests.

The best exercise you can do is ask your staff. They interact with your guests every day and are a great source of information. Now get a wide range of staff to ask and not just that person on your team who agrees with you. You want honest feedback, not just validation.

The Right Tools

Is your restaurant designed and equipped for the menu? It is quite shocking to see the number of restaurants in the new opening phase that have purchased equipment without even developing a menu. This is a great example of putting the cart before the proverbial horse.

Your menu has to work with the equipment and space you have. If you do not have adequate storage, it's going to be hard to be a fast-casual concept that focuses on freshness, especially with a large menu and limited space to prep and store products. Your team will do their best, but eventually, you might notice your turnover rate creeping up.

Is your cooking line designed with flow in mind? This is an element many owners never consider. You need to track the flow of every item on your menu from start to finish. How many stations does it jump through to get completed? How many people on the line have to add a component to finish the dish?

The more hands, the more possible problems.

Wording

Are you talking to the guest or down to the guest? Many a foolish chef has uttered these words: "The guest just doesn't get it." Exactly. You just hit the nail on the head and won the prize for discovering the obvious. If your guests don't get it, they won't buy it.

This is where ego and foolish pride trip up a lot of owners. It's easy to say you want to be "true to your brand." No problem. But keep in mind…

Brands change.

Many restaurants have closed their doors because of these shifts and because the owner could (or would) not adapt to the changing market.

You have a vision for what your restaurant is. Your guests have a vision of what your restaurant should be, and more importantly, what they will spend their money on. Somewhere in the middle is where your restaurant needs to be.

Goldilocks and the Menu

You know the story of Goldilocks and the Three Bears. This story is a great reminder to talk about the size of your menu. How many items are too much? How small can you go? These are complex questions that go hand-in-hand with additional questions that were mentioned earlier.

What is your style of service? Fast-casual? Full-service? If you want to be a fast-casual, then remember that the word "fast" is in the name. Now, the fast-casual concept is very popular, yet too many new restaurants jump on the trend without really thinking out the size of the menu. There are some that attempt to have a full-service-sized menu in their small, fast-casual space.

Not the best idea.

What equipment is on your line? If you don't have enough prep area, storage space, and firepower on your line, your menu might be too much for the setup you have.

What is your average ticket time? Slow ticket times are an indication of a few issues. The line flow might be not thought-out very well, and as a result, could lead to many bottlenecks occurring on the line (whether they be too many stations or too many steps toward the final dish), ultimately delaying service.

The team members themselves could be the issue if they have low skill sets, poor training, or lack of leadership. What skill level is your staff? Do you have experienced staff, or do you employ more first-time workers? Your menu can only go as fast as the team can keep up.

Data Tells the Truth

Your point-of-sales reports hold a wealth of data, that when extracted, analyzed, and acted upon, can be very profitable. You need to trust that process. Like a pilot who is trained to fly by instruments and not rely on what their eyes see, many restaurants have closed their doors because owners ignored the warning signs from their product mix reports.

Your reports tell you exactly what your guests are spending their money on. Listen and create menu items that are more in line with popular items. Stop trying to outthink or overthink the dynamics of your menu. The evidence is right there in your point-of-sale reports — drop the ego and pay attention.

Your menu should be like the line in that old Commodores song, "Easy like Sunday morning." If you struggle every day to manage prep production, orders, and ticket time, then it is time to ask yourself, "Is your menu too aggressive for your market?" If your answer is yes, then take action and make some changes.

The Menu Pricing Game

Strategies on Pricing Restaurant Menu Items

Menu pricing should be straight forward, yet it is rarely that simple. There are many elements you need to keep in mind when pricing out your menu. Let's explore the dynamics of menu pricing.

Real Food Costs

Too many operators live in the land of theory. They think that purchases divided by sales tell you your food cost. It gives you one side of an equation. The problem is, this process does not give you performance metrics to measure what is going on under the surface of your menu.

This is where the profits are hiding!

Knowing your food cost is not a luxury; it's a requirement if you want to have a chance at making money in an industry notorious for thin margins. To do this, you need one of the following:

- A food cost program (this can be as easy as an excel spreadsheet)
- A restaurant management system (like HotSchedules Restaurant Management Platform)
- An all-in-one point of sale system like the one by Toast

If you want to play the menu pricing game, you need to stack the odds in your favor. That starts at ground zero: know your costs. Precisely.

Commodity Pricing Model

Another major mistake is pricing your menu based on the competition. How do you know they know what they are doing? Perhaps their restaurant is always packed. But, are they making money?

If you can provide better service and products, why price your menu to compete? Creating value is more important than price. Many people get that wrong. They think that value is purely price-driven, and it's not. Value is created when you deliver those intangibles that add to the perception of value.

Stellar service, outstanding facilities, professional-looking staff, and the presentation of the food are part of the dining experience.

If you compete with other restaurants on price, you are a commodity. Pricing on the commodity level is a never-ending battle of lower prices. It's a game you cannot win in the long run. The only way to compete is to be cheaper. If your competition does the same, you both keep lowering your prices until you both go out of business.

Build value by embracing the spirit of hospitality.

Play to Your Strengths

Your menu needs to be a representation of what you do best. Think of your menu like your greatest hits album. The Rolling Stones recorded 439 songs. When you go to a Stone's concert, do you want to hear those "B side" tracks or just the hits?

Your menu needs to play your hits. Those are the items that will allow you to stand out from the crowd. That creates a brand differential. Having items that separate you from the others allows you to price your menu differently. Being different is good. Think of Apple. They sell computers, laptops, and mobile devices, like a lot of other companies. Being different allows them to stand out, create brand differential, and charge a premium for their products.

What the Market Will Bear

You need to do some research and conduct a competitive pricing analysis. Gather menus for your market and write down what is the pricing of a similar item from your menu.

Collect data from 5-7 restaurants in your market on a similar food item. You are looking for the high point; the low, and then figure out the average. Based on the "value" you bring what you can price your item for?

Take a hamburger in Albuquerque, New Mexico, drive up to Santa Fe (45 miles away), and you can charge $2-3 more just because the market in Santa Fe will bear it. Think about the last time you were at the airport and paid $5 for bottled water and $7 for a yogurt. When you have a captive audience, you can charge what you desire…to a point. If you price gouge your guests and they do not feel it was worth it, you'll lose them fast.

Menu Balance

The trick to winning the menu pricing game is to balance your menu with high and low-cost items. You can once again stack the deck in your favor by taking advantage of menu engineering principles and modern consumer psychology. Menu placement is critical to getting that balance just right. Think of your menu, like real estate. You have nice parts of town and places you don't go after midnight. Your menu is the same.

Finding the right balance is not an overnight process. It takes time to dial in a menu and get the balance right. At a minimum, you'll need:

- To keep your food cost accurate.
- A point-of-sale system
- An abundance of patience and focus

A new menu design can stimulate sales. A well-engineered menu will increase your profits! Sales without understanding your costs is a recipe for failure in the restaurant industry.

The cold hard truth is there is no one-size-fits-all menu pricing strategy. It has to take into account your brand, your market conditions, your overhead, your staff, and, most importantly, your guests. In the end, your guests will give you feedback if your menu pricing is where they want to spend their money.

Listen to them.

A Guide to Menu-Costing

The Real Food Cost Killers

When it comes to pricing out your menu, how did you go about it? Did you just pick pricing out of thin air as to what you **think** is appropriate? Did you call your friend who runs a restaurant and ask them? Did you look at another restaurant's menu and think to yourself, "that looks fair." If you did, it's okay. The menu pricing police are not coming for you (*although they should*).

Pricing your menu is part marketing (called positioning) and part science (knowing your numbers). When these two come together, you have a one-two punch that will set your menu up to knock out the competition. If you go only with one, you better be able to take a beating. The real food cost killers on your menu are not hiding in the kitchen where you can see them. Waste, inventory, and production are the low hanging fruit in the battle of food costing. *Easy wins.*

To call out the killers, you'll have to go to some places you may not have considered before.

No Market Comparison

When you fail to analyze the market, you are one step closer to becoming included in the yearly statistics of restaurants that close their doors. The reason many fail to do this vital step is what psychologists call **illusory superiority**. It is a cognitive bias many have that explains why many overestimate their abilities. You think you are smarter than the market and know how to price out your menu without data to support your decisions. *Sorry, you're not that smart.*

Do your homework. Look for an item that you might share. If you're an Italian restaurant, you probably have lasagna on your menu. Make five columns, and at the top, write down the names of the restaurants. On the left-hand side, write down the menu items and then start putting the prices down. *Where does your lasagna stack up? Are you the highest price, lowest, or in the middle?*

Wherever you are right now, the thing is not to jump to conclusions. Do not make any decisions yet because we need some more information. **Price alone is not what you want to make decisions on.** We are aiming for the elusive thing in marketing known as positioning.

Position Your Menu for Success

Positioning your brand in the market requires a knowledge of your market. Specifically, two elements you need to think about: is your market demand-driven or price-driven?

Demand-Driven Market: If you are in a smaller market, your restaurant concept might be pretty unique. Now, if you have a menu that truly stands out and there are few competitors you will find yourself in the position of being able to price your menu at more a premium if you can also deliver to what your guest perceives is a value (where service and food quality meet). Then you are more in control of the price dynamics. It's the golden rule: he who has the gold makes the rules or in economics terms: supply and demand.

If you are the only restaurant in your market selling Akaushi Burgers and "if" your guests are looking for gourmet burgers, you're golden.

Price Driven Market: You sell gourmet burgers, and so do a lot of other people. You do the market research of the competition and see that the most expensive burger in your market is $11. Because there is quite a bit of competition, you'll find it difficult to ask for $14. The question here is: *what will your market bear?*

Back to The Lasagna Price

To continue our conundrum about the price of your lasagna in the example earlier. You find your lasagna compared to others in your market has an average price point of $14. You want to price yours at $16. Should you do it? Answer these questions honestly:

- *Do you use better ingredients?* Papa John's made his brand stand out from all the other pizza places by marketing his famous "better ingredients, better pizza" tagline. If you are using the very best product that you can source, then you should be paid a premium. Here is the catch 22: you'll need to market that. You know you use the best. Your staff knows it.

  Does your guest?

- *What is your brand about?* Are you fine dining, fast-casual, quick service? These segments all carry a price perception that comes with them. It doesn't matter if your lasagna is the best in your market (all restaurants think theirs is), if you are a quick-serve restaurant at a food court, you will not be able to get the same price as a fine dining restaurant with full service and table cloths.

- *Have you costed out the portion on the plate?* Take a common item you have like lasagna. You or your chef see it on the plate and start making tweaks to the presentation. The portion is just a little too small, you think. It needs a cool garnish, maybe? How about spinach oil and fried basil? It needs more fresh cheese on top. Soon that awesome theoretical food cost becomes weighed down with a lot of hidden costs that you never put into the recipe, and now your price becomes a killer of profits.

Marketing effectively can help you overcome price positioning if you can show "why" you are different. If you get drawn into being on the lower end of the price positioning spectrum, then be ready for the "commodity war" ahead of you. Restaurants in the middle of the market (*also known as average*) get into pricing wars that devalue their brand. Human beings have a very natural tendency to be competitive, and once you get your emotions involved in pricing your menu, that's it, game over.

The real food cost killers are not hiding in plain sight. They are lurking in the shadows of not knowing your marketing, pricing by gut (not data), poor positioning of your brand, and not noticing all those "extras" that get put on the plate.

If you don't even have the fundamentals done (like costing out your menu completely), you should not attempt to price out your menu and expect to make money. If you do, congratulations, you have a hobby and not a business.

Menu Challenge: Order the Items with the Lowest Sales Mix.

Most restaurant leaders try the newest products on the menu and have favorites they always order. But sampling some of the least popular menu items gives a sense of what a product is like when the ingredients have been sitting around for a while and ask the question why this item is least popular? Are you up for this challenge? Write your observations in the notes.

The 3 Things Successful Menus Need to Be

Your menu is a lot of things. It's a marketing tool. It's a calling card. It's your brand. Too often, menus are not given the respect they rightfully deserve.

Your menu is more powerful than you may realize. It's the one thing you can almost be sure will be viewed when someone walks into your restaurant. Your menu sets the tone and expectations for the guest experience. In collaboration with your ambiance and your team, your menu is pretty much the star, and the rest are just supporting players.

There is a wide variety of options you must consider when designing your menu. There are three Golden rules that all successful menus follow. If you want to have an impact on your business that a great menu can deliver, abide by these three rules.

1. APPROACHABLE

Your menu has to be approachable from the viewpoint of the guest.

It's great to have signature dishes on your menu. You need them. They become your brand differential in a crowded market.

Keep it in English. If your guest is unsure about an item, the chances of them ordering it drop dramatically. Now granted, you'll have those adventurous diners who ask questions of the service team and will be eager to explore exotic ingredients on your menu. Most restaurants cannot survive marketing to a small niche in the market. Unless, of course, you are a celebrity chef and can command $100 or more for one of your tasting menus. If you are one of those chefs, then stop reading and get back into the kitchen to your foam canister.

2. CONTAINABLE

Many chefs and restaurant owners can design elaborate menus that can entice hungry patrons to come in and dine. The problem for many comes in the execution of such elaborate menus. Up until the guests take that first bite of your food, you have only talked a good game.

Menus need to be designed so that the culinary team can execute every item on the dish flawlessly. Large menus with complex plating details (like three different infused oils, carrot threads, and microgreens as a garnish) tend to slow kitchens down. Not paying attention to the number of items on the menu coming off each station is another recipe for disaster. If your menu has ten sauté items and you only have a four-burner stove (unless your sauté cook is the Flash), expect items to drag the station. Nothing hurts a menu more than poor timing in the kitchen. All the food needs to hit the window as close to the same time as possible. Nothing quite says we don't have our act together like serving half of the table and dragging the rest of the food another 15 minutes.

Function and flow should be a major consideration whenever you are designing a menu.

3. PROFITABLE

For your menu to turn a profit, you need to know the cost for every plate on the menu. There's no way around it.

With modern technology, there is no excuse why you can't monitor and manage your food cost. HotSchedules has a complete restaurant management platform that includes programs to help you manage inventory, control cost, schedule, recruit, train, keep online forms, a manager's logbook, and even analyze insights from your POS system.

Upserve POS is another industry disruptor when it comes to power to analyze data from your point-of-sale system with seamless systems built right into their software. Gift cards, loyalty programs, online ordering, customer relations management software are all built into one system.

Profitable menus don't just happen. They are carefully crafted, analyzed, and implemented with ruthless precision and accountability. Once your menu is up and running, it doesn't stop there. You need to constantly look at the data and make smart decisions about what items to add or take off. Your menu is your number one marketing and profitability tool. *Treat it with some respect.*

Here's a story that relates to menu design:

The Old Man, the Boy, and the Donkey

Let me tell you a story that pretty much sums up how most restaurants design their menu.

An old man, a boy, and a donkey were going to town: The boy rode on the donkey, and the old man walked beside him. As they went along, they passed some people who remarked it was a shame the old man was walking and the boy was riding. The man and boy thought maybe the critics were right, so they changed positions.

Later, they passed some people who remarked, *"What a shame! He makes that little boy walk."* They then decided they both would walk.

Soon they passed some more people who thought they were **stupid to walk** when they had a decent donkey to ride. So, they both rode the donkey.

Later, they passed some people who **shamed them** by saying how awful to put such a load on a poor donkey. The boy and man said they were probably right, so they decided to carry the donkey. As they crossed the bridge heading into town, they lost their grip on the animal, and he fell into the river and drowned.

The moral of the story? *If you try to please everyone, you might as well kiss your ass goodbye.*
That applies to your menu too, if it tries to be everything to everyone.

MARKETING

"The goal of marketing is not to make a sale. It's to keep your brand top of mind."

-Donald Burns, The Restaurant Coach™

The 10 Commandments for Restaurant Branding

There are a lot of moving parts that comprise a great restaurant. Outstanding service and food are part of that equation. The elusive element of branding, however, is a critical element that keeps restaurant consultants around the world steady with clients.

Let's look at your restaurant components like the human body. As the owner, you are the brain. You send signals to the rest of the body to keep it going. Your team is the heart of your restaurant. Your heart might not be 100%, and you can still survive (for a while). Profitability is the blood; your restaurant needs it to flow to keep alive. Your brand is like air. You cannot live very long without air.

Think of the following 10 Commandments of Restaurant Branding as if Moses himself brought these down from the mountain carved in stone tablets. If you violate these sacred things, then you risk the wrath of the restaurant gods and your customers!

1. ALWAYS PROTECT YOUR BRAND

This was a very important lesson I learned, working for Wolfgang Puck. Every business decision you make about your restaurant needs to always ask this question, "Does this enhance or detract from my brand?"

Are you adding a new menu item? Does it fit with your brand? Hiring a new employee? Do they fit with our brand culture?

If you want better results, you need to ask better quality questions.

2. BRANDS THAT DO NOT PROVIDE VALUE OR SERVICE DO NOT LAST.

Your brand needs to be "others-focused." Too many restaurants operate on what is easiest for the owners and employees and not on what is best for the guests. You might have the best food in the world, and you might get business because of it too. Your restaurant will not be in the hearts of your guests until you make them your focus.

3. NEVER DEVALUE YOUR BRAND.

Remember the words of The Joker in The Dark Knight, *"If you're good at something, never do it for free!"*

When you get on the "discount train," you are setting your restaurant up for failure.

Discounting also conditions your customers that you are willing to devalue your products. Why would guests want to pay $9.00 for calamari when they can get the same dish at $4.00 for happy hour? If you want to drive traffic at different meal periods, then design menu items that are a lower price point and are signatures for that time.

Half price on all appetizers during happy hour devalues your regular menu. A specially designed small plate menu during happy hour with creative items not normally found on your menu will drive business to your door.

4. YOUR BRAND NEEDS A STORY.... A GOOD FUCKING STORY.

People love a good story. Great brands embrace and tell their story to everyone! Who does not know that Apple started in Steve Job's garage? Is your meatloaf recipe handed down from your great, great grandmother? Do you only use Spanish olive oil to finish your pasta; because of a trip you took to Europe? Stories provide the human element of a brand.

5. ROME WAS NOT BUILT IN A DAY, AND NEITHER IS A GREAT BRAND.

It takes a while to build a brand, and this is where many owners fail. They expect everyone to fall in love with their brand as fast as they did. The truth is, very few brands are overnight successes.

You need to have faith and confidence in your brand even when times get tough. Trust me on this; you will question your brand. Not every day is going to be sunshine and rainbows. Now here is where many restaurant owners go astray. When the going gets tough, they wander away from the brand they created. They start to take advice from others (many have no restaurant experience), and the brand becomes "diluted."

Here is the one question you need to remember, "If you don't know what your brand is, how do you expect your customers to know?"

In the 80's movie Top Gun, Tom Cruise's character loses faith in who he is. He is overconfident. When thrown in with world-class pilots, he starts to doubt himself. He soon learns there are rules he needs to live by to embrace the culture of excellence that combat pilots need to be the best of the best. He develops a saying that he repeats over and over to himself, "I am not leaving my wingman!" You need to develop a similar mantra, **"I am not leaving my brand!"**

6. YOUR BRAND MUST STAND FOR SOMETHING. IF YOU DON'T STAND FOR SOMETHING, YOU'LL FALL FOR ANYTHING.

Brands that have a cause find a niche that connects customers quickly. People like people who are just like them. Consider the restaurant that has an outdoor patio and allows dogs. They provide water bowls and house made "dog biscuits" for patrons. They connect with a group that has shown if you love my dog, I'll love your brand.

7. CONSISTENCY IS HOW GREAT BRANDS THRIVE.

Inconsistency is the slow death of any business. If you allow an attitude of indifference to grow with your service team, don't be shocked when they treat your customers with the same nonchalant behavior. If you allow your cooks to take shortcuts and compromise the standards, do not be surprised when your customers go online to write reviews on the inconsistent food.

8. YOUR BRAND MUST CONNECT TO THE EMOTIONAL SIDE OF PEOPLE.

Behavioral scientists will tell you that it's in our genetic makeup to be social creatures. Great brands understand and take advantage of what was mentioned earlier as "the human element." Take a look at commercials for cologne or perfume. There's no way by watching a TV commercial that you know what that product is going to smell like. They flash images of beautiful people, doing beautiful things in beautiful locations. Those images stir up emotions. Emotions sell things. Period.

Restaurant brands can play into a wide array of human emotions like romance, adventure or style. A small intimate restaurant could say, "Our restaurant was voted number one most romantic views of the city. Rekindle that spark with dinner reservations tonight at Chez Paris."

Humor is another great emotion that restaurants can tap into. How about a pizza restaurant that puts a social media post up saying, "You had me at mozzarella." or at staff wearing t-shirts that say, "Legalize Marinara." People connect with brands that don't take themselves too seriously. To paraphrase a famous Marilyn Monroe quote, "If you can make someone laugh, you can make them do anything."

9. YOUR BRAND MUST EXPLAIN "WHY" YOU DO IT.

Simon Sinek has an amazing book entitled *Start with Why*. He discusses the concept that most brands focus on telling you what they do and how they do it. Sinek goes on to explain that great brands explain why they do it. Marketers love to throw out the words *brand differential* or unique selling proposition. Most restaurants can adequately describe what and how they do to stand out from the market. Great restaurant brands connect at the emotional level of why.

Here's how Chipotle does it. "We believe that food should not only be fresh, but it also should not contain hormones, antibiotics, or GMOs. We believe your food should be prepared in front of you so you can see our commitment to using fresh, local, and sustainable products. We also make a damn great burrito." When you explain the why behind what drives your restaurant, you'll stand out so far in the market that others will be playing catch-up.

10. IF YOU DON'T STAND OUT FROM THE CROWD, YOU'LL BECOME PART OF THE CROWD.

If you have followed closely to the previous 9 Commandments, then this one is just icing on the cake. Have a great story that explains your why. Connect with the emotional side of people and deliver value. In your brand promise, be consistent, and customer-focused. When times get tough, you need to believe in your brand. If you follow these Branding Commandments, you'll find that your restaurant definitely stands out from the crowd.

How Social Media Is Changing for Restaurants

Unless you live in a cave or on a deserted island, you would have seen the impact social media has had upon the world. For the independent restaurant, it has become the dragon slayer you can use to market against the big brands. You do not need a multi-million-dollar budget to be effective on social media. However, you do need to be smart, clever, and have a game plan.

Too many restaurants just randomly post on social media, thinking that is what social media marketing is all about. It's not that easy. You need to have a few pieces in place if you want to be able to market against the Chipotles of the industry.

Model Others

If you want to save yourself some heartache about social media marketing, the best thing to do is to model the businesses that are getting results. Take a look at some of the restaurants in your market that are getting big numbers, and dig deep into what they are doing and do something similar. But that does not mean you imitate? It means you should look below the surface.

What emotional triggers are they employing? At the heart of it, marketing is all about triggering emotions. Understand that, and you'll open up a door to more likes, shares, and comments. People want to be moved to action. If you're putting up the same boring posts about your daily lunch or dinner feature, you will just get lost among the thousands of other restaurants in your market doing the same thing every day. You need to go beyond the hunger emotion. Tapping into different emotions is vital to successful social media marketing for restaurants. You need to have a palate of emotions to tap into. Think of it as the seasoning for a recipe. You don't just rely on salt and pepper for every recipe. Sometimes you need to throw in some saffron and cayenne!

Many restaurants play the humor card, and for some brands, that is a good one to play. Look closer at your market profile (otherwise known as your avatar) to uncover more emotional triggers.

Your avatar is an exercise where you dig deep to create an imaginary character who buys your product. The more detailed you can be about the ideal person you want to attract to your business, the more effective your social media will be."

Now your restaurant might have a primary avatar, and you'll have secondary ones as well. The main thing you have to realize is that your restaurant cannot be everything to everyone. That is a recipe for failure. It's better to be something to someone. Being in a specific niche is the ideal. Dominating that niche is your goal!

Understand the Hierarchy

There is always a hierarchy of social dynamics. It's the way of the world. Social media is no different because not all social media posts are created equal in the eyes of your fans. Know what your guests want and give them more of what they want (not what you think they want), and you'll unlock key number two to social media success.

The Written Word

Plain posts with text and nothing else sit at the bottom of the hierarchy. When social media first started, this was about the only thing you had. However, times are changing, and while words can still be powerful, they are usually looked over.

Even Facebook realized this and has a new feature that makes short word posts (35 characters or less) much bigger than normal text. Facebook calls this feature "dynamic text," and it will draw attention back to simple word posts. It's a challenge to get your point across in just 35 characters.

Pictures

They say a picture is worth a thousand words. That is true if it's the right picture that reinforces the message. Make sure the pictures you post-trigger emotion or show emotional elements. Pictures of your food are great if well done. But sadly, too many restaurants post pictures of their food that are less than desirable. Some of the best pictures you can post are of your guests having an amazing time at your establishment. Nothing sends a message like a photo of people having fun.

Also, go behind the scenes and give your online fans a look at the culinary team in action during service. People love a look "behind the curtain" to see the edge of the restaurant industry, so boasted about infamous books like the late Anthony Bourdain's *Kitchen Confidential.* When you do post pictures like this, try using a black and white filter to enhance the tone.

Pictures with Words

The next level up is to place text over your photos. *Happy Birthday, Happy Anniversary,* or even the name of the dish goes a long way to boost a normal picture and get more views. People have become a little lazy when reading posts, and this helps them make a faster decision about whether or not they want to read further.

GIFs

Aww, the GIF (or graphics interchange format file). Unless you are still hiding in that cave we spoke about earlier, you would have seen these. Simply put, they are pictures that move. If you think a picture is good, sometimes a GIF is better. Even Apple has made using GIFs easier by allowing you to search and add one in iMessage.

You might love them, or you might hate them. But here's the thing: millennials like them. Why? Because they connect to the way we're wired to communicate – nonverbally. Research has shown that 55% of how we communicate is nonverbal. GIFs make that happen. You say you're excited about your new dessert menu? Add a GIF of a girl jumping up and down, and now they'll get the emotion behind the words. That's powerful.

Video

If a picture is worth a thousand words, then a video is worth a million! Now that most people own a smartphone, anyone can post videos online. Before, you would have had to hire a crew to come in, record, and edit your video for online consumption. Now, you just hit the button, record, and share!

Video is a massive tool for leveling the playing field against big chain restaurants. If you are creative and daring enough you can create a video for your brand that has the chance to go viral. How powerful would it be to capture a once in a lifetime event like a couple getting engaged in your restaurant? How about shooting a video of the chef at the local farmer's market talking about the incredible produce?

Sadly, video is not used by a lot of restaurants to get their message out to their market. But if you want your brand to dominate and not just compete, then you need to post more videos.

Know That the Demographics Are Changing

When social media came out, most people were very selective about what they posted. They would only share pictures that made them look their best. We went from collectors of memories to sharing in the moment.

Today, social media posts are much more spontaneous. Millennials will share random short videos on Snapchat of their breakfast, or use a filter to give themselves dog ears and a tongue. Social media is changing for sure, and we, as an industry must make adjustments to change with it. We need to speak social media in the way that our guests communicate.

That means dropping the façade and becoming real. Tapping into human emotions and letting people know the faces behind your brand.

Be accessible.
Be real.
Stand up for a cause.
Support a charity.
Be proud of your team.
Be a member of your community.
Be funny.
Be an authority.
Be iconic.

Be human.

4 Tips for Taking Your Restaurant's Social Media Game Higher

If you are in any restaurant or coffee shop, look around. You'll notice people on their smartphones, tablets, or laptops.

Being online and connected to social media is our new addiction. It's said that the average American spends about 19% of their day, or around 4.7 hours, on some form of media.

That is very exciting for restaurants!

Yes, it is said that we tend to spend more time looking at our phones than we do at real people. But the good news is that your restaurant has a very captive audience. They sit there, waiting to be attracted to your social media posts. You need to break away from the same old stuff you have been posting and break away from the crowd of mediocrity.

Here are four tips for taking your restaurant social media game to a higher level so you can start impressing your customers (and attracting plenty of new ones).

1. GO LIVE

If you want to take your social media game to high levels, you have to know two words: Live Stream.

As social media gets bigger and faster, you'll need to do more than make your posts attention-grabbing. You need to make them shareable! Live video streams are that vehicle to get your brand noticed. One big platform that's making a splash is Facebook Live. You can also stream live today on Instagram, Twitter, and LinkedIn! **It's a live world, and you need to be a part of it!**

Video is more about being spontaneous and showing what goes on behind the scenes. While you'll want to take more time when composing food pictures, for video, you want a little more off the cuff. You could have a question ready that you want to ask your staff like, "Tell us why you love working at Joe's Diner?" Then hit the button and go live!

Is it going to be perfect? Probably not! Is it going to be real? **Definitely.** Live streaming lets people share in what's going on in real-time, and that is what people find appealing. If you're nervous about going live, you can go "semi-live" on platforms like Snapchat.

Be bold.

Maybe live stream a cooking class or maybe a behind the scenes look at a menu planning session with the culinary team. Let people see the fun. Let them see the chaos. Let them be a part of the experience!

Use a call-to-action.

Get on the video feed and ask people to come on down and check it out for themselves. Too many social media posts are flat, in the sense they never ask for the guest to take action. If you have exceptional food and service, don't be afraid to ask them to come on down and join you! These will also work up to 24 hours after posting if you use Snapchat and/or Instagram Stories.

Be consistent.

With live stream video, you'll have a live channel to communicate with your guests. You can even name it to give it some credibility and get a nice following. Maybe there is a *Chef's Table Live* stream in your future? Just make sure to stay with it and have broadcasts regularly. Nothing worse than getting people excited about something and then dropping the ball.

There is comfort in taking action. As the famous tag line from Nike goes... Just Do It! You have to jump in and get going. If your teenage kids can do it, so can you!

2. BETTER PHOTOS PLEASE

Smartphone users have increasing expectations for new features, and manufacturers like Apple and Samsung have delivered.

Take advantage of these to give pictures of your restaurant depth.

For example, the iPhone 10 and 11 have a portrait feature in the camera mode that allows you to focus closely on a subject as it blurs the background to give more texture and contrast. This allows you to really showcase the action of your restaurant.

Look at the colors on the plate. So many pictures on social media are monochromatic, and the colors seem flat and lifeless. You want pictures that stimulate the senses and warrant a second look. Steak with roasted potatoes and brown Demi glacé are all too close in color for your eye to take notice. Thus, they usually get overlooked in social media streams very easily.

Use natural light when possible because it gives the best overall look to pictures. A dark dining room with fluorescent lighting might make a great dinner atmosphere, but it tends to taint photos of food and people with a yellow hue. No thanks.

3. POST MORE

Now, this might go against what some "social media experts" would say to do. However, you have to look at the vastness of the internet and understand that if you want to create a buzz about your restaurant, you must stay at the top of mind on social media feeds. That means upping the number of posts you make a day.

The typical restaurant posts maybe once a day. That's like throwing a pebble in the ocean and thinking you are going to make a wave.

You're not.

You need to tap into the true power that social media has by using the synergy of three platforms: Facebook, Twitter, and Instagram. If you are not using all three and using them consistently, then get a bucket full of pebbles are start throwing them into the ocean of social media. You will spend a lot of effort for very little results.

Use a social media management tool like Buffer to help you analyze the data. You use your POS system to help you run a better and more profitable restaurant–right? Why not use the data from a social media management tool to help you be more effective with when to post your social media?

Without social media management, you would be just guessing and hoping that what you are doing will work. Remember that hope is not a strategy.

Data will tell you when your posts get the most traction and views. Just like the data from your POS system, you take that information and create more things like that.

Don't be shocked when you see the data results. You might think that posting at 4 pm is a great time to get people to know about your features for the night, and then the data tells you that more people see your posts at 10:30pm! Adjust your restaurant's social media strategy and post things at night so that they can get more views and more likes.

Social media is not about making a sale. That needs to be repeated: *social media is not about making a sale.* It's about keeping your brand top of mind.

You want to be seen as "the choice" in your market. Take a hint from the major brands that advertise on traditional formats like TV. Do you see only one Little Caesar's Pizza ad a week? Oh no. That commercial gets into your subconscious until you are singing that tag line, "Pizza, Pizza" like a parrot!

Here is a good way to start: whatever you are posting now, double it!

4. USE HASHTAGS RELIGIOUSLY

The hashtag is used as a filing system for the internet. You need them attached to every post you have.

Three rules about hashtags:

- They have to be relevant
- They have to identify your brand
- Don't go crazy - too many hashtags clutter up a post and make it seem like excessive ramblings.

Keep the hashtags controllable at up to three per post, or else you end up with a post like this.

"Make sure you swing by Donald's Pizzeria for dinner tonight! It's BOGO night - buy one large pizza, get another for just $5! #hashtag #restaurant #chef #dinner #eat #pizza #foodislife #Boston #myrestaurant #chefsname #beer #feature #wickedfood #whynot #getdownhere #DonaldsPizza #onemorehashtag"

See what I mean?

If possible, research your hashtags too. When you type in a hashtag on Twitter or Instagram, it will tell you how many times that hashtag has been used. You want at least one hashtag that is very popular, so your post will be included in that search. Once you have one strong hashtag, you'll want to create a unique one for your brand if you are a taco concept, maybe something like #CarpeTaco to show off your passion to Seize the Taco!

The last hashtag should always be your brand name. Yes, your name is on the user account. However, you want to start building your name up on the internet as a searchable tag. That means every post gets your brand name.

Game On!

Taking your social media game higher is easier when you raise the bar and make a commitment to push it beyond your comfort zone.

Playing it safe might be good for the average restaurant. Average restaurants don't get noticed and don't get buzz generated about them.

Social media is a powerful tool for restaurants that have the guts to tap into it and harness the power. You can make noise and be seen, or you can stay in the shadows with the majority. As it is with so many things in life, you have a choice.

What are you prepared to do to get your restaurant noticed?

4 Ways Independent Restaurants Can Outfox Big Chains

The chains are coming! The chains are coming! Okay, take a deep breath, it's not that bad. Many independent restaurants look at a major food chain coming into their market with fear and panic. They should look at it as an opportunity to market their differences from the big corporations.

While the chains have the upper hand when it comes to a big marketing budget, there are some clever ways to negate this threat. Play to your strengths. Showcase the things that make you different. Chain restaurants have a complex system for change that is their Achilles' heel. The battle between chains and independent restaurants can be compared to the epic story of David versus Goliath. We all know how that turned out for Goliath.

Here are four key ways to outfox the corporate giants:

1. PLAY THE LOCAL CARD.

Unless the corporate chain was founded in your town, this is a huge advantage. It's one you should play every day. You're local; they're not. There is a huge trend, or should I say more like a demand for restaurants to utilize local ingredients. That philosophy should be taken further for communities to support local restaurants.

Local economies thrive when revenues are produced and spent in the same community. That is a sustainable economic structure. Use that to your advantage.

Also, being a smaller operation allows you to make changes much faster than big corporations. Is there a hot trend out there that you see as having potential in your market? As an independent, you do not need to wait on a board of directors or a committee to implement changes. Being small means you can move faster.

2. FIND A CHARITY TO SUPPORT.

Another way to stand out in your market is to find a local charity to stand beside. Now, many big chains also support charities...big charities. The local softball team, food bank, animal shelter are hometown organizations looking for support from their community. Step up and become their fan, and the community will, in turn, support your restaurant.

Remember to look at community-based organizations and not ones that focus on religion or moral compass deviations. We have all seen the backlash on the internet for restaurants that refuse to bake a cake for a gay couple (one in Indianapolis closed their doors and one in Oregon has been ordered by a court to pay $135,000 in damages). Remember, with the internet, word of mouth is now "world of mouth." Not all PR is good PR.

3. ENGAGE ON SOCIAL MEDIA.

When guests comment on one of your posts, say something! Follow them back on Instagram and like some of their posts. Social media should follow an 80:20 rule. 80% of your activity should be commenting on and sharing their posts. 20% should be about your restaurant.

There is an app that notifies you when a VIP guest is walking in your restaurant, called Wisely (www.getwisely.com). This app takes your normal loyalty program and puts it on steroids. Imagine being notified when a VIP guest walks through the front door. Now you can greet the guest by name or alert your staff to the guest's arrival. You can build a preferred status tier, just like the airlines and hotels do. As the guest racks up points, you can offer exclusive benefits like priority seating, extended happy hours, complimentary amuse bouche, and chef's tasting menus.

That is hospitality.

4. CREATE A SIGNATURE.

The last thing you want to do is compete head-to-head with a big chain on one of their signature items. Just because Buffalo Wild Wings rolls into town, does not mean you now need chicken wings on your menu.

It is always better to create signature items. A good recipe for developing a signature item looks like this:

- **1-part Brand Story** - a family recipe or something from your original menu.
- **1-part Local** - incorporate a locally sourced ingredient or historical name/place.
- **1-part Flavor** - any signature item you create has to deliver on taste.
- Mix well and deliver through social media.

Post pictures of people enjoying your signature creation (that's called social proof), get guests to write reviews, get out there, and tell your community about it.

When you have a winner, brag about it.

Being flexible to make changes is your secret weapon. Being local is your calling card. Creating signatures that no one else has is your ticket to outfox the big chains when they come calling to your market.

Being an independent is your strength.

The Alteration of Social Media Communication

By 2020 it is estimated that there will be around 3.28 billion social media users around the world. It is estimated that the average person spends about two hours per day using social media. You need to know how to reach them.

If you want to be successful in breaking through the noise in today's social media-obsessed world, you need to speak this language. Times are changing, and if you want to get out of the middle (it's always too crowded in the middle anyway) then let's take a look back at the evolution of social media and the alteration of its use.

Your Parents Facebook

On October 24, 2003, Mark Zuckerberg had an idea for a kind of "hot or not" game for students at Harvard to compare students from rival dorms. He called it Facemash. Unfortunately, the university shut him down within days of the launch claiming a violation of copyrights, breach of security, and violating individual privacy for stealing the student pictures (he hacked into their dorm sites), which he used on the site.

A mere four months later, in February 2004, Mark Zuckerberg relaunched a new social media platform for Harvard University students that he named the facebook. He soon offered it to a few other "Ivy League" colleges, and the site took off virtually overnight and has not stopped since.

Back then, Facebook used text and photos to communicate. Mobile phones were not as internet friendly as they are today, so mostly the way to post was through a computer. We collected photos, and we carefully selected which ones to share. Back then social media was more "deliberate."

How you can maximize this platform:

- **Always include a picture with a post.** Our brains are wired to pick up visual cues. That's how most of our ancestors avoided being eaten by wild animals. That being said, your picture has to stand out! Throw words on there that capture the emotions you wish to capture. Bam! Wow! Yes! These are words that will invite the follower to look again.

- **Increase your posts.** Most people worry that posting once or twice a week is too much. It's not. Social media is like the size of the ocean, and if you post a few times a week that would be like taking a rock, throwing it into the water, and expecting a big splash. Good luck with that. You need to experiment and see what the threshold is for your demographic. You do that by pushing the limits, and when you get some feedback, you push a little further than that! Don't worry if you lose a few followers along the way. Just like your brand cannot be everything to everyone, neither can your social media strategy. You want to target the center and not be as concerned with the outliers.

- **Be social.** Make sure to track your response rating on your page and make a conscious effort to keep it above 90%. Remember that the real secret to social media is to be social. Reply when people comment. Wish followers Happy Birthday if they are friends of yours. Take the focus off yourself and more on the people that like your page!

Say Hello to the Microblog

It seems people had a thirst for smaller messages on social media, and the microblog got its real push into the mainstream with the birth of Twitter in 2006.

Twitter and other microblog sites provide a way for people to communicate quickly, share news, and connect in a very fast-paced venue. With Twitter, social media took another turn as it became more on-demand and instant communication between brands and customers. Most major brands have a presence on Twitter these days, and if you don't it's not too late.

Wendy's has even reached the national news level due to its Twitter feed. The company targets those that maybe don't have great things to say about the hamburger chain and they pretty much "roast" the person with a witty and often very clever come back!

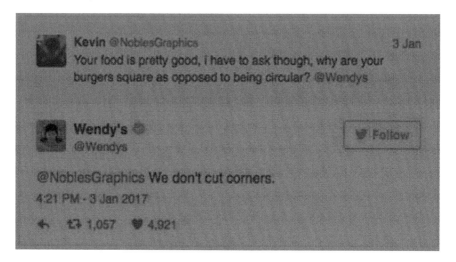

Old school Twitter was a challenge to convey your idea in just 140 characters (luckily that has been raised to 280 characters). For some, Twitter has a real appeal. To condense your thought down to its bare essential elements. For years, the platform held tight to its rule of character limits until recently when it released the restriction on photo attachments and now does not count your picture in the word count. That is great news for brands that want to employ the power of visual elements to their message.

How you can maximize this platform:

- **Use a graphic.** Like mentioned before, a picture is worth a thousand words. Use that to let your brand stand out.
- **Retweets are gold.** Yes, you need to be social here too! Check out the Twitter feeds of your followers, and if you like what they post, give them a heart at the minimum a retweet is what they call the real "social currency." When you pass along good information or a funny tweet, you get credit for being on-trend or funny as well.

- **Have a persona for Twitter.** You want to have an agenda and a voice for this venue. Like your menu, you cannot just be a hodgepodge of random thoughts. Keep it dialed in. If you are passionate about sustainable food sources, then follow those experts that talk on the subject, follow them and retweet their posts. Use the "quote tweet" feature to add a few of your own words to back it up and reinforce your persona.

Is That a Picture of Your Breakfast?

For those that like to express themselves through photos and short videos then Instagram is the platform for you! Launched in October 2010 this platform found a home among users across multiple generations. Now Instagram is unique in the sense that you can only upload and share photos or videos from your mobile device. You can see them via the Internet on your computer; however you'll need the app to post.

Instagram's appeal is that it's visual and very fast. Just tap the picture twice to give it a heart (which is the same as an Internet high five). They also have 23 different photo filters that you can apply to give your post a touch of your style. These filters helped transform ordinary social media communication into extraordinary.

Instagram, along with Twitter has become very popular with celebrities, and it allows us to have behind-the-scenes access to their life and thoughts. You don't even have to be friends with a celebrity to follow them. High profile hospitality professionals like Danny Meyers and Wolfgang puck both use Instagram as a platform for promoting their brands. You should take advantage of promoting your brand as well.

How you can maximize this platform:

- **Show behind-the-scenes.** Take some tips from celebrities and give people an inside look at your restaurant. Use different filters to add a dramatic flair.
- **Show your human side.** Brands by themselves can be rather cold, so you want to humanize this by showcasing your staff and the guests who frequent your restaurant.

- **Have fun with it.** Instagram has some cool video apps that can turn average video into something fun and interesting. **Hyperlapse** allows you to create a professional-looking time-lapse video. **Boomerang** takes a burst of photos and weaves them together to produce a little mini video that plays forwards and backward. **Layouts** allow you to make a little photo collage of multiple images to a single post. You can add from two to nine photos.

Where are the Millennials?

If you are wondering where the new generations are hanging out on social media, you need to head over to Snapchat. In 2016, this platform struck a chord with the Millennials and Generation Z. You see, social media has gone through an evolution over the years. We have gone from being selective to what we share (collectors) to an era of instant expression.

"Look how that jerk parked their car." Snap. Take a picture and post it.
"Hey, check out these cool boots!" Click and share.
"These are the most amazing tacos in the world!" Selfie time.

Add that Snapchat allows you to take a short video and build what is known as a "story" (each snap disappears after 24 hours), and you have the hottest trend in social media — *sharing your life through video.* Think of Snapchat as a messenger app on steroids!

Now, the other social media platforms are trying to catch Snapchat with the instant expression game and have all introduced live video features. Instagram recently launched their own "stories" feature (some will say it's a direct knock off of Snapchat) as well as an Instagram Live. Facebook and Twitter both now offer live video features. Whether you are a fan of live video or not is not the issue. The point to take home is that a big portion of your guests do like video posts. If you want to have a chance to market them to draw attention to your brand, then you are going to have to jump on the video bandwagon. *NOTE: the new social media platform that is getting a lot of buzz is Tik Tok. You should check it out and see if it is a good match for your brand.

Here are some tips for breaking into video posts:

- **Take the jump.** With the incredible optics included on most smartphones today, you have a portable video studio right in your pocket. No need to hire a big film crew or buy equipment. Just take your phone out, hit record, and post. Boom.
- **It's not going to be perfect.** The whole key to instant expression is to be authentic and a little spontaneous. Don't try to craft out a 20-minute monologue on why you think porcinis are the king of the mushroom family. Keep it short. Keep it simple. Keep it to one topic. Remember that you're dealing with a society plagued with attention deficit disorder, so keep your videos more like small snacks.

As social media evolves, we must evolve along with it. Too many restaurant owners get hung up on the past and talk about "the good old days." Let's face the fact that the good old days are gone, and they probably were not as good as you think they were. Our minds have a twisted way of storing information. Have you ever heard someone tell a story about something that happened and your thinking to yourself, "That's not the way I remember it?" It's okay. It happens more often than you think.

Everything changes.

That is a law of nature. You can do what we do best as humans and adapt, or you can remain in a time bubble trapped in the past. It's a new era in social media marketing. Things that worked five years ago on social media, barely have any impact today. You have to constantly update your strategy and stay current with what's hot out there. Social media works if you use it smart and consistently.

Video marketing is the new frontier.
Those that dare to embrace it and
use it will catapult their brand.

3 Reasons Your Independent Restaurant Needs a Marketing Plan – Right Now!

Marketing is a big buzzword that gets thrown around. We all know we should have a marketing plan. But guess what? Most restaurants don't ever put one together, and that is what is killing the independent restaurant. So, if it is so important to long-term brand success, then why do so few have one?

The number one reason is, they don't see the value in creating one.

If your brand is the heart and breadth of your business, then marketing would be the air you need. Marketing is more valuable than you realize. Let's explore why you need to jump on the marketing wagon today.

1. MARKETING IS THE GREAT EQUALIZER

Marketing has not always been affordable for the small independent restaurant. Unless you had the multi-million dollar budgets of large chains, it was very difficult to hang with the big boys. Then the social media revolution came along, and the entire game changed. Marketing is now a silver bullet to fight competition on a playing field that is easier to conquer.

If you can be creative, you can capture the attention of millions on social media. Is it easy? No. Can it be done? Yes. The key is to dial your marketing in on emotional triggers.

Make marketing multidimensional. Understand the way people are consuming content. Jennifer Smith, account director at Restaurant Social+, a company that specializes in restaurant marketing for restaurants, says, social media is evolving.

2. MARKETING IS COST-EFFECTIVE

Billboards, print ads, and direct mail are still out there. They are becoming outdated because of the way we now consume information through mobile platforms.

The money it would take to run a billboard for three months could be used more effectively with targeted Facebook ads, and if set up correctly could pull people into your restaurant today. Think about how many billboards you remember from your commute to work today. It would be safe to say that you might struggle to think of any that stood out and made you want to drive to that restaurant today.

Then there are apps like Waze (the world's largest community-based traffic and navigation app) that can drive guests to your front door. Geo-targeted ads on Waze pop up when guests are close to your business, it shows them your offers, and with the push of a button, will give them directions to your business! For the right restaurant concepts. That can be very powerful marketing.

Most social media marketing costs nothing more than your time to create and post. Creativity is the key and getting out of the same boring mindset that most restaurants stay in. So, if marketing on social media is so great, then why do most restaurants do the same thing? They are stuck in their comfort zone.

People get stuck because they listen to those voices of doubt in their heads.

"My guests aren't on social media."
"Social media is not for me."
"I don't need to market. I rely on word of mouth."

Word of mouth is now world of mouth with a single click of a button. Your restaurant can reach more people with more frequency and with lower costs than ever before. You need to jump into the pool and start swimming.

3. MARKETING KEEPS YOUR BRAND TOP-OF-MIND

More and more restaurants open every year. Some analysts suggest that we are approaching a restaurant bubble that will burst within the next few years. With more restaurants clawing for a piece of the market, you'll need to not only keep the standards high within your restaurant; you'll need to keep your brand what is known as "top of mind."

That truly is the goal of marketing: It's to keep your guests thinking of you over the competition. That's why using multiple social media platforms is so critical to a well-designed marketing plan. You need to use at least three platforms to get what I call is the Triad Effect. There is synergy in using multiple platforms.

You might use Facebook as your primary; however, you can boost that by also incorporating other platforms like Twitter and Instagram. Now, you'll need to do a little research to find the perfect triad for your restaurant and market. Once you find your "power three," you can create a yearly marketing plan to hammer your message into the subconscious of your target demographic (known as your avatar). This is the only way your brand will survive the burst of the restaurant bubble coming.

Marketing, like having outstanding food and service, takes two things: commitment and consistency. You cannot have effective marketing without a plan.

The Real Business of Restaurants Isn't Food — Its Emotions

What do you sell? Think about it. What is the driver behind "an experience"? It's emotion.

We are, by nature, emotional beings. It's the depth of our emotions that make us human. We have a wide range of emotions we can tap into. They can elevate us to the highest levels, or they can take us into our lowest lows.

You can't ignore the power in playing the hunger emotion. It can be a primary driver in the reason guests come to your restaurant. While the hunger card can be like holding an ace in your hand during a poker game, and although it is nice to have, you would not want to go all-in on a single ace. You need supporting players to be able to deliver the winning hand in the game of restaurants.

EMOTION: CARING

Human beings are emotional and also very social. We gather in groups and communities to form a collective bond that carries us through the best and worst of times. Think of towns like Boston that become a fan frenzy when the Red Sox win the World Series. Look at how the town came together in unison for a tragic event like the Boston bombing.

The sense of community is one that pulls people together. You can tap into that by supporting your community. Pick a local charity, youth group, or animal shelter (furry friends are family, too!) and do some marketing towards helping one of them out. You have to be a good neighbor before you can be known as the neighborhood restaurant.

EMOTION: ADVENTURE

If you're like most restaurants, not everyone in your market is local. Tap into the emotion of adventure guests crave when exploring new restaurants, new flavors, and local ingredients. When most people travel, they want to eat like a local.

What locally sourced ingredients or farms could you spotlight on your menu in your social media to help you stand out in a crowded market? New Mexico is famous for its green chile. In the fall, roadside vendors fire up butane tanks and baskets full of freshly harvested green chiles that are flame-roasted right in front of you. Some tourists become so addicted to the flavors that they find restaurants and farms that will ship them to their homes.

EMOTION: CERTAINTY

While we discussed that we need adventure, we also need certainty, for something familiar. When you tap into this, you have a menu item that can become a top seller.

Comfort food says it all in its first word: comfort. Deep down, we have memories and feelings of food from our childhood. Those are hardwired into our subconscious and get triggered when we see certain words, such as meatloaf, grits, fried chicken, stew, pierogi, tamale, posole, picadillo, or matzo ball soup. Depending on where you grew up, some of these words might trigger an emotional feeling of being home. Home is always an emotion you want to tap into.

EMOTION: SCARCITY

This emotion has been employed by advertisers for decades because it works. "For a limited time only" is often the tagline used. Missing out is a powerful driver that you can use more in your menu design.

Many restaurants use happy hour menus to draw people in before dinner. These menus are specially priced to entice. While it is a great concept, most restaurants execute this incorrectly by offering items from their regular menu at a discount. By doing this, you have now just devalued the item.

If you created a special happy hour menu with unique items that your guests can only get during that specific period, you now have a limited time offer that can drive sales and keep your brand value intact.

EMOTION: SURPRISE

Sometimes that little something extra, a little something that comes unexpectedly with a purchase, can go a long way. It could be at the beginning of the meal, such as chips and salsa, or perhaps an amuse-bouche appetizer from the chef. It also can transcend beyond food, like providing purse rack setups by the table for ladies. Even just having mouthwash in the restrooms can be a nice surprise.

Explore the concept of "take-home marketing." Give a treat (cookies, truffles, etc.) that the guest can take home. Make sure the box or bag has your logo or branding on it. Then later that evening or the next day, the guest will see it, and it will trigger a positive emotion about your brand (if you exceeded expectations during their time at your restaurant). This is how you create raving fans with unexpected surprises.

EMOTION: CONNECTION

This is probably the most powerful of all marketing emotions. When people feel connected and feel a part of your brand, you have something few can buy — loyalty. Brand loyalty is the reason people will drive past a dozen other restaurants to dine at yours. When your guest feels connected, you don't compete in the middle any longer.

You stand out.

Now you have some emotions to tap into beyond just the one of hunger! When you are willing to change your view of marketing and the guest experience, you will open up your brand to a bigger world.

Stop competing, and
you will stand out.

MINDSET

*"Once your mindset changes,
everything on the outside
will change along with it."*

-Steve Maraboli

3 Reasons Your Restaurant Plan Isn't Working

All good restaurateurs make a restaurant plan - but what happens when that plan isn't working out?

When you open a new restaurant, people will flock to check out your new venture. You'll have visions of grandeur about your restaurant being everyone's new favorite place.

Then, the people slowly stop coming back, and sales start to drop. Doubt sets in.

If you have ever owned, managed, or even thought of opening a restaurant, you need to accept that doubt will pop up when things get tough. The critics in your head love to make an appearance when things don't go as planned.

That's life, and as tough as it is to hear, there is a huge obstacle in the way of getting your restaurant to where you want it to be. That obstacle looks back at you every morning in the mirror.

This might be a hard pill to swallow for some. However, if you truly want to excel in this industry and reach your potential, then grab a big glass of water and get ready to choke this down.

Your Restaurant Plan Needs Adjustment

The greatest strength you have is your ability to change. If you want to keep getting the same results, keep doing the same things. It does not take an Einstein to figure out that when you are not getting the results you want, then *you need to adjust your restaurant plan.*

The hard part is admitting that things are not working the way they are now. Maybe - just *maybe* - you made a few mistakes with your restaurant plan.

But don't get down - mistakes are your greatest opportunity for growth. Embrace them.

ADJUSTMENT #1: BRAND POSITIONING

Is your brand positioned properly? Positioning is a key element to successful marketing. It is how your restaurant is placed in the mind of the guest. To truly succeed, you might need to adjust how you see your brand in your current market.

There is a vision of the restaurants that you have, and there is a vision of your restaurant that your guests have. Somewhere in between is the restaurant it has to become.

Are you trying to fit a square peg into a round hole? Sure, with enough marketing money, you can force your positioning into a market. It's much easier to adjust to the market instead of having the market adjust to you.

Some people see a successful restaurant as being lucky. Some do when they position their brand properly and find it connects with their market. If your restaurant is not doing the numbers you'd like, then it's time to think about how your brand is perceived by your market.

ADJUSTMENT #2: PRODUCT MIX

Your product mix report is a gold mine of information if you take the time to extract the data.

Smart restaurant operators are always aware of how their menu items are selling because this can impact your product mix. Let's say you want to be a restaurant that is known for its delicious steaks. However, when you look at your product mix report from your POS, you see that most guests buy your fried chicken and meatloaf. Does that mean you stop selling high-end steaks? Not necessarily. But it means you should take a closer look at your product mix.

No one likes to hear that maybe their restaurant plan needs to be adjusted. It hurts the pride and ego. But would you rather be right or be successful?

"There is a vision of your restaurant that you have, and there is vision of your restaurant that your guests have. Somewhere in between is the restaurant it has actually to become."

Donald Burns, The Restaurant Coach™

Your Staff Needs Replacement

Water seeks its own level. Like attracts like. They are a lot of metaphors that convey this message. There are also quite a few reasons your team is holding your brand back.

1. **You do not have a culture that attracts top talent.** This is another hard concept for some restaurant owners to hear. Do you treat your team in the same manner as you want them to treat your guests? Your team will treat your guests the way you treat them. This is called modeling and it's hard wired in our DNA. We learn our behaviors from others. As the owner or leader your behavior is the example that your team will adopt.

2. **You have some bad hires and you kept them.** Now, if you are being the leader you should be and they still are not performing to your standards, then you have a team member that has some behavioral issues. That can be extremely hard to change. They basically have picked up some bad behaviors and habits that hold them back and no matter how great your culture is and how amazing your restaurant is. Some people just are not a good fit for your brand. In most markets, there are a few restaurant options and it's better to let those that are not a good fit go work for another restaurant that could be a better fit for them.

Letting people go is never easy. Especially in this business we tend to be around our staff for extended periods of time. Lines can become blurred between friends and coworkers. That makes it difficult for some to discipline and enforce standards. If you want to be a real success in this business, then you need to separate the two. It's far better to let go of an employee that has become your friend who might not be a good team fit, then to let poor performance continue and risk not only your brand but also the friendship long-term.

Not everyone is a good team fit. Understand that and have respect for the welfare of your brand.

Your Attitude Needs Improvement

What do you fear? The truth will set you free after; of course, it pisses you off. Many restaurant owners and managers overcompensate to avoid facing their fears. Your fears can keep you stuck and held down from reaching your potential. Even the wise Yoda reminded young Luke Skywalker that he must, "Named must your fear be before banishing it you can."

Overcoming your fears is one of the most important lessons anyone must face if they are going to maximize their true potential. Restaurants truly become better when the people in them become better people. So, take a minute to reflect and think about what you fear. This exercise can be terrifying and exhilarating at the same time.

It's so easy to get stuck in a negative attitude. Maybe sales are not quite where you want them to be. Perhaps you lost a few key employees to the competition. Or maybe a couple of bad online reviews just put you into a funk. Whatever it is, you need to let it go. Negativity breeds negativity. As a leader within the organization you must maintain a positive attitude.

Your attitude has a contagious effect on the culture of your brand. That culture has a trickle-down effect on everything from team performance, ambiance, and eventually the guest experience. Lest we forget that in the restaurant industry we don't sell food and beverage... We sell an experience.

If your restaurant plan is not working the way you want it, then you need to modify and update your plan. Things change. Markets change. Your restaurant must change too. Just remember that all change starts with you.

From Manager to Restaurant Leader in 10 Vital Steps

Congratulations, you got the promotion! Whether that's because of your hard work, discipline, and tenacity, or because in a heated battle the previous restaurant manager walked out, you are now in charge.

However, chances are, no one trained you on *how* to be an effective restaurant manager. Many people in this predicament fall back on modeling the behavior of past managers they have worked with… good and bad.

Act like those terrible managers from your past and you become like them. There is a better way. There should be a higher standard for restaurant managers to contribute to the culture of your restaurant and to lead the staff to higher goals of service, output, and positivity.

Here are ten steps to making the shift not only into management but into leadership.

1. TAKE PERSONAL ACCOUNTABILITY.

From this day forward, you are responsible for the results you get. That's right: it's time to drop the "blame game." Leaders step up and take responsibility for how their team performs.

If someone drops the ball, a manager might ask, "Whose fault is it?" However, leaders will ask better questions about accountability, such as, "How can I train this person better, so this does not happen again?" When you ask better questions, you'll find that you get better results.

2. YOUR CORE VALUES ARE YOUR COMPASS.

Core values are the building blocks of any business culture. Knowing your core values is a big step towards becoming a leader. Here is the other side of that equation, though: you also need to *live* your values.

Managers can be very hypocritical when it comes to "walking the talk." Leaders, on the other hand, say what they mean and do what they say. This key component alone will rocket you towards leadership because it builds trust with your team when you do exactly what you say. Integrity is not something that can be bought; it's a core value you live.

3. TEAR DOWN THE WALLS.

The restaurant industry is notorious for the divide between the Front of the House (FOH) and the Back of the House (BOH). Leaders understand that all work is teamwork, and restaurants need every team member focused on the bigger picture. Allowing the petty attitudes to grow is a recipe for failure. You need to stop it and reinforce the culture of what the word "team" really stands for: **Together Everyone Achieves More.**

4. INVEST IN YOUR PERSONAL GROWTH.

It's true: school is never out for the professional. All top achievers and leaders commit to continued learning. The average American reads around 17 books per year. The average corporate executive (CEO) reads 4-5 books per month!

You can argue that there is no relationship between learning and earning, but the facts say otherwise. Check out these must-read restaurant management books. And if you don't have time to read, there are other ways to feed your brain the good stuff, like listening to audiobooks, taking online classes or attending seminars. A leader is focused on making themselves better, so they can make their team better.

5. TAKE CARE OF YOUR BODY.

We all know the hours in the restaurant industry can be brutal. If you want to lead people, you need the energy to do so. Energy comes from applying "self-care" to your routine. That means eating smarter, drinking plenty of water, getting a good night's sleep, and exercising.

If you want to throw out the excuse that you "don't have time," I want to point out that you have all the time you need. You do not make it a priority. If something is a "should," it will happen if all the elements involved line up. If you make it a "must," then you will make it happen. **Managers "should" all over themselves all day long. Leaders take action and make it happen.**

6. ALWAYS BE TRAINING.

Leaders understand that repetition is the mother of mastering any skill. Malcolm Gladwell suggests in his bestseller, Outliers, that there is a 10,000-hour baseline of practice that separates the amateur from the true professional. How many basketball free-throws do you think someone like Michael Jordan has done? One of the primary jobs a leader takes on is consistently training the team. How you train is how you'll perform.

7. THE DEVIL IS IN THE DETAILS.

What is the difference between a manager and a leader? A manager is thinking and working two steps ahead of the team. A leader is thinking and working *20 steps* ahead of everyone else. Stepping up to leadership means also taking steps to make sure you are organized, on track, and on schedule. You need to adopt a system that allows you to track information, notes, and keep on top of all the little details that come with being a leader. You can go old school with a paper planner or get everything you need on your smartphone. Here are some great apps to get you rolling:

- Evernote– a cloud-based note-taking app that does it all!
- Things – a productivity app that allows you to organize projects and create the action steps to make it happen.
- Dropbox – a cloud-based file storage site that gives you one place to put all the recipes, documents, pictures, MP3 and PDF files that you need to run your business. You can share these files with a simple click.

8. GO FROM ONE-DIMENSIONAL TO FOUR-DIMENSIONAL.

Becoming a leader means understanding what makes people tick. Most people assume that everyone else functions and is motivated the same way they are. Nothing could be farther from the truth. Understanding behavioral dynamics is what separates the leaders from the managers. You need to understand people... all different kinds of people. The first step is to take a behavioral survey for yourself first. You need to understand what makes you tick before you can start to understand others. Then, you can move on to the members of your team.

There are quite a few different behavioral surveys on the market that can teach you about yourself and others. The DiSC® Assessment is a very popular one for businesses, and there is a lot of information on the internet to explain the different behavioral traits. The ProScan® Survey is another one that not only measures a person's natural strengths but also tells you the kinetic energy a person has. Think of kinetic energy as your natural battery; it gives insight into a person's ability to handle multiple tasks and challenges.

9. BE GRATEFUL.

True leaders are thankful and grateful. They know that with synergistic teamwork, the ordinary becomes extraordinary. Leaders are always telling the team and their customers that they appreciate them and are grateful for what they bring to the business. When was the last time you told someone sincerely that you were grateful for them? Leaders know that when they put out positive energy, they get even more returned to them. Cultivate an attitude of gratitude and watch how your world changes.

10. STEP OVER THE LINE.

When you become a manager, you step across an imaginary line of going from one of the "hourly" to that of salary. When you crossed that line, you unknowingly took an oath to protect the owner's interest. Many restaurant managers have a problem with this and do not want to be seen as "the bad guy/girl," trying instead to maintain the same relationships they had with other team members. It never works. When you take the position, you'll need to step up your game if you want to stay on that side of the line. The best way to step up is to commit to becoming a leader.

Leaders never go backward. They only move forward.

If you find yourself in the position to become a restaurant manager, only take it if you are willing to make the changes needed to become a leader. The restaurant industry needs more leaders who live life by a set of core values, have integrity, are grateful, and are committed to becoming more than just average.

The best example is this: a manager stands behind his team, points and says, "Go there." A leader stands in front of their team and says, "Follow me."

Restaurant Coach Story

After my service, I did what many young chefs do...I bounced around from restaurant to restaurant. If I was learning, I stayed. If I felt they had nothing to teach me, I moved on. Then one day, I was working at a restaurant in Miami, and the chef (Peter) pulled me aside to talk. "You have some raw natural talent."

Now, I had heard that on many occasions from my father; however, I always dismissed it as his attempt to do some father-son bonding.

Chef Peter continued: "I hate seeing talent go to waste."

Me: "What do you mean, Chef?"

CP: "You have talent, yet you don't push yourself. If you continue, you end up like Dave over there, just a CLC." (A CLC is a Career Line Cook, the older guy in the kitchen who is just a culinary Mercenary. No real passion that drives them anymore because they gave up on their dreams. Now they just come to work and grind it out. They are very good at what they do. However, being good is an excuse to stay comfortable)

There are those times when you know what to do, yet you don't do it. Then there can be that moment when everything clicks and that internal switch is flipped. Like when I was holding the wall during crossovers. Chef Peter's words flipped that switch.

Knowing what to do is very different than doing what you know. Talent and skill might get you to the top; however, it's discipline and character that will keep you there. My martial arts training gave me discipline. Being a Pararescueman forged my character. I had to get back to basics.

My military Spec Ops training made the restaurant business a natural calling. That chaotic dance during service that can push many over the edge was calming to me. When lives are on the line in a military operation, you are trained to stay calm and focused. They call it Front Site Focus. You are aware of the total situation around you, yet you are focused on one target at a time. When the restaurant became busier, I became calmer, almost like a slow-motion video playing in front of me. Clarity and focus became my edge.

After that talk with Chef Peter, I started using the tools that my time in Spec Ops taught me. Those tools not only work for specialized military operations, but they also work in the restaurant industry.

I share these same Spec Ops Mental Management Tools with my restaurant coaching clients. They might not know it, but they are training their mind to work for them instead of against them.

The 12-Step Solution to Your Sales Slump

It's natural for a business to be up and down. We call it the cycle of business, and we accept it. However, what do you do if your restaurant sales are down and seem stuck there?

Here's What Not to Do

1. PANIC

It's hard to be calm when you see your sales trending down with no sign of relief. The last thing you want to do when your sales dive is to react. Reaction is pure emotions driving the bus. You do not want emotions to drive your business. It makes for a great reality TV episode, but it's not good for brand stability.

2. GET DESPERATE

The desperate restaurant owner is a sad sight to look at because it can result in a compromised brand. It's usually in this very vulnerable state that a "friend" suggests trying this or that. The problem is, this "friend" has never owned a restaurant, and most are not restaurant experts except for the fact that they eat out often. You try their idea, and maybe it works… for a few days. You may try another idea, and that works for a few days, and then another, and so on.

However, soon, you notice that the few loyal guests you have are not coming back. You see one of them on the street. You mention you have not seen them at the restaurant and then they drop the bomb on you by saying, "you've changed." Welcome to brand drift.

Brand drift is when you have changed so much that the original elements that made your restaurant great are barely visible. It comes from being desperate. You have drifted away from your original brand identity and are lost. If you don't know what your brand is, how do you expect your guests to know?

Here's What to Do: The 12-Step Process to Increase Restaurant Sales

Take a look at the **anatomy of the guest experience**. There is a process that every guest that comes to your restaurant experiences. If you take a look at each piece of the puzzle, you will uncover the ones that could use a tune-up.

1. **The Prescreen:** The first thing you need to know is that your customers are using cell phones and social media to find out if you are worth their hard-earned money. They will look at Facebook, Yelp, Tripadvisor, and Google to get a better idea of who you are. Make sure your menu is updated on your website and across any social media channels where you might have it posted. People reading your menus online can get hooked on the idea of having that certain dish - only to be extremely disappointed when they get to your restaurant find out the menu is different.

2. **The Entrance:** The customer experience starts in the parking lot. Be aware that some things might be beyond your control, like the lines in the parking lot. To the guest, these little things start a chain reaction that can stack the deck against you if you do not monitor them. Every shift, a staff member should do a complete walkabout of your property to see things from the guests' point of view because that's the only point of view that matters.

3. **The Dining Room:** Now we get into setting the tone for the customer experience. Look around your dining room and imagine seeing it for first time. Try to pick up on some of the things that might throw a guest off. Chipped paint, worn-out carpets, and tired décor send a signal to the guest that your heart is not in it. In the mind of the guest, perception is projection. If they think it's true, it becomes true for them.

4. **The Greeter:** This is the first real interaction that the guest has with someone on your team. Believe it or not, a lot of negative guest experiences are due to this touchpoint. *The greeter sets the tone.* You need to have high-energy, outgoing, and personable staff up front - this is where putting the right people in the right position is paramount. You cannot easily train people who are not happy and do not naturally smile.

5. **The Server:** This is another critical position and one that you need to hire for personality over skill. *Service can be taught* - it is just the mechanics of the dining experience. Serve from the left, clear from the right, and so forth. The missing element is hospitality. That's the human connection. It's what takes service and elevates it to a higher level. Hospitality is a feeling, and the restaurant business is truly a business of emotions. If the greeter sets the tone, the server reinforces it.

6. **The Table:** Now that their order has been taken, the guests will start to settle in. Whatever tone you have set up until this point is going to be amplified by what the guest sees while sitting at their table. If you've set a negative tone, then they will start looking for little things that reinforce their impression of your restaurant, like food under the tables or un-bussed table-tops. The sad thing is, we're six steps into the cycle of service, and they have not even had your food yet. For some restaurants, those are tough odds to come back from, no matter how great the food turns out to be.

7. **The Food:** The moment of truth. The first thing the guest will take in is the plate presentation. The brain is wired to process pleasant and appealing objects. They say that we eat with our eyes and it's very true. Remember that comment earlier that perception is projection? It rings true when the food is placed in front of the guest. You have to make the food look good, and then you have to back it up with flavor.

8. **The Check Back:** Here is where busy restaurants start losing points again. Having a presence on the floor is critical to elevating the guest experience. Your team needs to understand the difference between service and hospitality. Hospitality is an art, and it requires constant attention to the needs of the guest.

9. **The Manager or Owner:** Human beings have a need for significance. We crave acknowledgment and praise, this is hardwired in our DNA at birth. There's nothing quite like human interaction with customers, especially if it comes from an unexpected face like the owner, chef, or manager. This adds something special to their visit that won't be easily forgotten.

10. **The Busser**: Yes, the busser. This position is a key player in helping solidify the guest experience. It's disappointing because the position is often overlooked and not well-trained. Many times, the busser will have direct interaction with the guests when they ask the most common question, "Where's the bathroom?"

    Make sure your bussers are dressed in a uniform that is clean, neat, and meets the standards of your brand guidelines. Baggy jeans hanging down might make them look cool to their friends, but it makes a negative impression on most of your restaurant's guests.

11. **The Restroom**: Nothing can take a pleasant dining experience and turn it around, quite like dirty and poorly stocked restrooms. Some diners are known to furiously storm out of a restroom looking for a manager because the bathroom was out of toilet paper. There are plenty of pictures on online review sites of restroom fails - don't let your business become one of them.

12. **The Goodbye**: Here is your final chance to leave a great impression with your guests. Nothing is as powerful to humans as saying these two simple words - **thank you**. Research has shown that the last thing the guest remembers tends to form the foundation of the memory from their dining experience. It's called Recency Effect. Always finish the guest experience with a highlight, not a disappointment.

Problem Solved!

Everyone is looking for new ways to stimulate restaurant sales and drive more business. The great restaurants are constantly focused on the fundamentals. School is never out for the true professional. You train, and then you train some more, and then you train some more.

Maybe your sales have slumped because you lost touch with the fundamentals. The best way to recover from slow sales is to take a microscope to your existing operation - step-by-step - and make sure you're doing everything you can to ensure an outstanding guest experience.

The Real Enemy Within Your Restaurant Business

Human beings love antagonists. It's a classic storyline of good versus evil. We love it in books and entertainment. We also see it throughout the restaurant industry.

Back of the house versus the front of the house. The day staff versus the night staff. Your restaurant versus the one across the street. The list goes on and on.

Pointing out the bad guy gives most people an excuse for why they cannot achieve the level of success they desire. Maybe you have heard or even said some of the following:

- "It's my customers. They don't understand my concept."
- "It's my location."
- "It's my staff. I don't seem to get good people."
- And the grand prize winner goes to, "It is what it is."

No, it's not. It is what you allow it to be.

There is a classic African proverb that goes, "If there is no enemy within, the enemy outside can do us no harm."

Translation: *You* are your own worst enemy.

For some, that might be a hard pill to swallow. However, it's a great start. As aptly pointed out in the quote at the beginning of the book, "The truth will set you free, but first it will piss you off."

The only thing holding your restaurant back is you. *Talent and skill can take you to the top, but it's your character and mindset that keeps you there.*

Here are a few things about *you* to adjust if you want to see a positive change in your restaurant.

1. CHARACTER

Knowing your core values is a vital step to understanding who you are, what you believe in, and what you stand for. A lot of restaurants place most of their focus on systems.

Checklists, processes, and standardized recipes are needed to maintain consistency and accuracy. However, if the people using the systems do not have the right character, then it's all for nothing.

As the leader, your main role is to set the standards high and reinforce them through your actions and words. Otherwise, people will quickly recognize when you're phoning it in.

Body language accounts for 55% of how we communicate. The old axiom, "It's not what you say, it's how you say it," is so true. We are hardwired to the clues that nonverbal actions provide. A good standard to set for your staff is "do as I do, not as I say." If you see slackers or negative attitudes, you'll know who's responsible.

2. INTEGRITY

One of the most important character traits you can develop is that of integrity. Lack of integrity is one of the main causes of brand dilution and team destruction. To have integrity, you first have to be honest and true with yourself. You have to honor your commitments and your word.

> *"Lack of integrity is one of the main causes of brand dilution and team destruction."*

What happens when your guests find out they've been lied to? You tell yourself, your people are your most valuable asset, yet you call them names and degrade them in front of the team. Do you know why your turnover is so high? You are constantly on your team about keeping stations clean and organized, yet your office looks like an episode from "Hoarders."

If any of these are the case for you, do you now understand why your team does not follow directions?

Many people think that leading or managing is about saying the right things, or that being a great restaurant leader is just about inspiring and motivating the team. Words do have power. Used properly, words can have an impact on others… for a little while. It's when your words and your actions are in alignment that you will find the leader within.

3. MINDSET

Think of your mindset as the lens you use to view the world. So, if you want to change the way you see the world, change the lens, and everything will be great, right? Not so fast. While it's easy to make changes on the surface, the real challenge is those nasty things called habits that will trip you up.

Because your habits lie in your comfort zone, you have to break out of it if you want to change your mindset. Understand this: everything you want for your restaurant and your personal life is just beyond your comfort zone. It takes courage to change. It takes effort to change. Above all, it takes a *commitment* to change. Here are some wise words from Abraham Lincoln.

> *"Commitment is what transforms a promise into reality. It is the words that speak boldly of your intentions. And the actions which speak louder than the words. It is making the time when there is none. Coming through time after time after time, year after year after year. Commitment is the stuff character is made of; the power to change the face of things. It is the daily triumph of integrity over skepticism."*

> - Abraham Lincoln

4. MOMENTUM

A body in motion stays in motion. A body in bed stays in bed until the alarm goes off for the 10th time.

The best way to build momentum is to take action. It takes time to change patterns of behavior and willpower. Small, consistent actions every day can help rewire your brain for success.

Unlike the common to-do lists (which are not very effective), making a solid commitment to just three things are the perfect way to build the momentum you need. The CommitTo3 app allows you to set up teams and have accountability partners, which might be the push you need to get going.

There is nothing quite like the sweet taste of success. Once you've had it, most want more. Success in anything is a series of small tasks, and actions that done consistently will keep you out in front.

Remember that the restaurant business is about people. It's about knowing your core values. It's how your words and actions work incongruence. Your restaurant is a living thing that you mold and shaped by the actions you take every day. Good or bad, your restaurant is a reflection of you!

Defeat the Enemy Within

Your restaurant will only progress when there is a true leader at its helm - someone who can admit their flaws and work to better them for the sake of their staff, customers, and business. With the right character, integrity, mindset, and momentum of a true restaurant leader, you'll defeat the real enemy within your restaurant and see enormous improvement.

Black Belt Test

The year was 1981. I was 16.

I stood there in my white karate top that was covered in blood...my blood. I was almost through my first-degree black belt test, and I had one more round to go. I had completed all the katas, demonstrated the advanced techniques, weapons demos, three-step sparring drills, chin-na, board breaking, free sparring rounds with the 18 students that were testing that day, two and three on one sparring, and I had sparred with all the guest black belts that my instructor invited that special day (there were 8 of them). Now, the last thing I had to do was spar with my instructor, Terry L Bryan.

Sifu Bryan was a Vietnam Veteran. An Air Force dog handler who grew up in Texas. Karate in the Lone Star State is rough. Sparring down there back in the '70s was more of a full-contact street fight. You didn't get a black belt by not earning it. My instructor was going to keep that tradition. In most karate schools, you paid (sometimes handsomely) for your black belt test. At Sifu Bryan's studio, there was no fee; you had to prove yourself worthy to wear that black belt.

I knew I had to face all the students that day, plus, the two and three on one fighting. I also anticipated the other black belts that wanted to break me in on my quest. My strategy was to pace myself and save my energy for the black belts ahead. Fighting two or even three on one is not very complicated; you just want to use one as a human shield. No problem. Get through to the black belts with some energy reserve.

About three student fights into it, and I was dodging and toying with the students trying not to burn too much energy. A young girl, Marie, who was testing for her brown belt didn't like my tactics, thinking it made her look bad for her test. She grabbed my GI (Karate top), which by the way she wasn't supposed to do, and firmly punched me right in the nose. I was already sweating profusely, and I just thought that the warm feeling on my face was perspiration. It wasn't. It was blood...my blood.

I used my sleeves to wipe my face, and soon it stopped. Then the next student entered to spar, and now my face became an open target. They would get the bloody nose flowing again, I would wipe it with my sleeve, and the process just continued for the next hour. By the time I got to the black belts my strategy was quickly changing to more survival mode. So much for best-laid plans.

By the time I faced Sifu Bryan, I could barely keep my hands up. He had been my instructor for the last four years, and when I looked across the line, he was standing behind (three feet away), he had a look of pure determination in his eyes. This was not a look you want to see staring at you. I will never forget it to this day.

When the referee said "fight," I expected him to come at me hard. I did not expect a jumping front kick into my chest that knocked me off my feet and into the crowd about 6 feet behind me sitting on chairs. I remember laying there on the ground thinking, "Nice, I get a break for a minute." Oh no. My instructor was pushing people aside to get to me. He started to stomp down on me like he was trying to put out a fire! I was exhausted, and then something inside of me just clicked. I found that reserve energy that is triggered when you stop playing, and you fight for your life. I knew he had a bad knee, and so, I kicked him right there. It caused his leg to buckle, and I next kicked up as hard as I could into his groin. It picked him up off the ground, and he fell. I got to my feet as quickly as I could and moved back into the fighting area. This time I was ready. Hands up. Eyes locked — total focus.

Now I thought,"I am a dead man." I just pissed off a world champion karate expert by kicking him as hard as I could in the nuts. He got up, and yep...that look he gave me at the beginning of the match was kind compared to the rage in his eyes now. I wiped the blood on my sleeve one more time. I looked right at him and waved my hand to "come on." He closed in slow and steady like a tiger getting ready to crush his prey. I was ready. I was confident. I dropped the fear. His sidekick was easy to sidestep. I countered with a ridge hand strike to his ribs. He countered with a spinning back fist that I just barely avoided. I took a few steps back to gain distance and assess his vulnerabilities. Hmmm, that kick to his knee must have had some impact, because he usually led with his right leg and now he switched up to southpaw. Not his strong leg. A short stop kick to the front leg would give me an opening. I thought to myself, "Okay, this is it. Ready, set...."

The referee jumped in and said, "time." The fights are just two minutes each. I am not sure how long I was on the floor defending myself from him. It must have eaten up more time than I realized. We bowed to each other, and he wrapped his arms around me in celebration. I tried to embrace him back; however his grip was so strong my arms were pretty much pinned to my sides. He said into my ear, "I knew you had it in you. I will always believe in you. I wanted to see if you could go to that dark side when you had nothing left."

In the month before my black belt test, Sifu Bryan and I were training harder than ever. At one sparring session, he hit me hard with a right cross that put my head into the wall of the studio. It cut my left eye (still have the scar today), and blood ran down my face. I wanted to stop, and he told me words that have been a constant reminder to me when shit gets real and I am on the edge of wanting to stop. I had a towel on my face and was bent over leaning against the wall. Sifu said, "We need to finish the round." I gave him the look of are you fucking kidding me? He leaned forward and said, "There will be times when you will want to quit...don't. Always go a little further. Get past the impulse to stop. You always have more than you think you do."

He was right. We finished the round.

Back to the black belt test.

I had done it — my first-degree black belt in American Kempo Karate. My father who attended my black belt testing had always been a tough man of few words. He walked up to me in my blood-soaked uniform and gave me a compliment the only way he knew how "I'm proud of you. If I was getting beaten that badly, I would have come back with a gun and shot them." Uh, thanks, father.

The celebration party that evening was held at Sifu Bryan's house. I sat on the sofa with an incredible awareness of how drained my body was. Everything was sore (even my eyelashes). Marie came up and apologized for hitting me in the nose. We grilled burgers and watched our favorite movie, Enter the Dragon with Bruce Lee (I honestly have watched the movie over 100 times). Sifu walked over to me, handed me a beer and said, "This will help take the edge off some of the soreness." I sat there and rethought about the test and the moment that flipped that switch inside me. Laying there on my back with Sifu stomping down on me, I was afraid. I was immobilized by fear. Something deep inside of me screamed, "Fight! Kick him in the leg!" That voice was right. **Fuck this. Fight. Get up.**

That voice has become my friend who shows up when fear or overthinking wants to stop me. Some call this part of you, your dark side. Oh, and if you don't think you have a dark side...trust me, everyone has a dark side. It's that voice that wants, that desire, that craves more from yourself. The things you don't want others to know, the things you keep to yourself, those thoughts exist with your dark side.

Your dark side doesn't have to be evil. The difference comes down to this question: *Do you control your dark side, or does it control you?*

Your dark side is your alter ego. Superman had one. Batman had one too. When you control your dark side, you have access to powers you have deep down that you would never know existed. They are there, asleep, and just waiting to be unleashed. When you control it, you are unstoppable. When it controls you, you're reckless and out of control (some might even say you're a hot mess). The sun can blind you, or you can focus that raw energy through a piece of glass to create heat that can burn the earth. You'll need to learn how to harness your dark side into relentless power.

Too many people suppress their dark side. That's a mistake. It has unparalleled energy that can not only get you to the top of your game; it will keep you there! Some let their dark side out yet cannot control it, and they rage, yell, and throw tantrums. When your dark side controls you, trouble is not too far ahead. It's your core values and morals that keep the leash on your dark side. Without those two, your dark side will be a monster that reigns hell upon those around you. I've seen it first-hand. There have been times when I let out that dark side, and it controlled me. It cost me more than just money. It cost me, friends and family.

Having ways to connect with your core values every day is critical to keep you in control of your dark side. You never want to tame that force to the point that you cannot call on it when you need it. Too many suppress their dark side until it becomes a little kitten instead of the beast it naturally is. You do want it on a strong leash. It's controlled by those values and morals you set as your playbook for life. To succeed at anything, you must know the rules or expectations for the game. Use them to keep you in control of YOU!

The 7 Deadly Restaurant Sins to Avoid

On the surface, running a restaurant seems relatively easy. New restaurants open every day. It's estimated that over 4000 new restaurants open every year. If you're looking for a simple formula for restaurant success the recipe would be something like this:

- Provide great food in a clean, inviting atmosphere.
- Offer attentive, professional service that focuses on guest satisfaction.
- Market your brand across a variety of media platforms.

Then why do so many restaurants fail? It's quite simple: they ignored the seven deadly restaurant sins that are the demise of restaurant dreams of grandeur.

Running a restaurant is (in theory) relatively simple. It's the mindset of the owner or operator that is the chokehold to growth. If your restaurant is not operating at its maximum potential, then take a look at the following and see if you are guilty of any of these restaurant sins.

1. IGNORANCE

Contrary to the popular saying that ignorance is bliss, it's not. Ignorance is just ignorance. There are a lot of duties and details involved in running a successful restaurant. Many operators purely focus on the things they like to do. You can easily identify problem areas in any restaurant operation by using the word "should."

"I know I should cost out my menu."
"I know I should start an Instagram account."

"I know I should fire the manager who drinks in the office."

Most restaurant operators just "should" all over themselves. The tipping point in a restaurant is when the owner or operator turns their "should" into a **must**.

2. MEDIOCRITY

Remember the bell curve in school? It's based on The Law of Averages. Many restaurants in today's market live in the middle of that bell curve. It's the addiction to average that is killing most restaurants. The sad thing is that most restaurants are capable of becoming outstanding. Think about it. All restaurants have access to the same products, the same labor pool, and the same marketing channels.

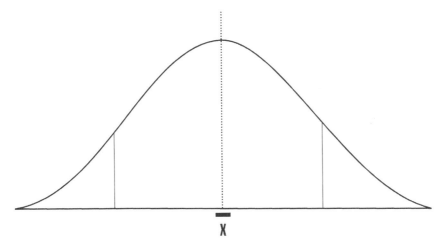

X

Why do some thrive and others survive? No one opens a restaurant thinking to themselves, "I just want to have an average business." No. They want to be great; they want to stand out; they want to be a huge success. Then, they faced a few challenges. They ran into a few obstacles. Then slowly they started to compromise on their standards. They sold out their integrity, and after that they headed down the path of mediocrity.

Quite simply, they settled and stopped pushing themselves.

The easiest way to stop that downward spiral is to raise your standards. Reposition the bar for what you will accept and for what you will not tolerate. Stop selling yourself so short.

"The saddest thing about selling out is just how cheaply most of us do it for."

- James Bernard Frost

3. PRIDE

This might be the sin that has closed more restaurants than a bad economy. Its common partner is ignorance. Together, these two work to stop the growth of the business. Many restaurant owners have closed their doors thanks to foolish pride.

Even the Bible calls pride one of the original Seven Deadly Sins. Yeah, it's that bad. When you allow your pride to override growth and opportunity, you're pretty much done.

Successful restaurant owners and operators are always looking for the opportunity to increase production, quality, efficiency, operations, and profitability. That requires conviction, confidence, and respect.

Pride, when inwardly directed, is a negative impact on your business. Pride, when outwardly directed, builds teams and communities and pulls people together. The problems come when we use pride to close the door to opportunity and growth.

4. FEAR

Look in Wikipedia, and it will define fear as a "perceived danger or threat." There is a common acronym for the word fear:

False
Emotions
Appearing
Real

Fear is another deadly sin that stops restaurants from growing. Even Luke Skywalker had to face his fears before he could become a Jedi. So too must restaurant owners face their fears if they wish to maximize their potential.

Here are some statements I've heard from restaurant owners based on fear:

"I can't fire that person because I'll have no one to work."
"I can't change my menu without losing customers."

Fear needs to be recognized and acknowledged. Say you can't fire that person who is bringing your team down and driving your customers away? **Yes, you can.** Get on the internet and recruit until you have ten interviews set up for tomorrow. It's better to have two superstar employees than a dozen losers.

When you surrender to fear, it becomes your master. It controls every business decision you make or are afraid to make. Just remember that while danger is very real (fire, tornado, etc.) …. **fear is a choice.**

5. ENVY

Some restaurant owners let this sin become all-consuming. They are so focused on what other restaurants in their market are doing that they lose track of what is happening in their establishments.

Granted, you need to understand what's going on in your market. However, becoming obsessed with what the restaurant down the street is doing to the point that every time they make a change in the menu, you feel you have to add a similar item to your menu… could be a little overboard.

Just because every restaurant in town has a flatbread appetizer on it, does not mean you need one too. Sometimes being a little on the outside is a great way to differentiate yourself in the market.

6. GREED

With all the talk about raising the minimum wage, this is a good opportunity to talk about the sin of greed. Successful restaurant owners and operators understand that you truly get what you pay for, both in product and with talent.

If your restaurant is set up properly, you can pay the overhead, pay your team, pay your vendors, and still walk away with a good profit margin. Restaurants that pay their staff higher than average wages have less turnover, increased productivity, higher guest satisfaction scores, and less waste and theft.

Smart restaurant owners plan with yearly budgets and then manage their team to reach those financial outcomes. The old saying is quite true, "if you fail to plan, then you are planning to fail."

7. BAD HIRING

An entire book could be dedicated to this sin alone. Who you allow on your team to handle your perishable product and interact with your guests is one of the most important decisions restaurant owners and operators make.

Here are some of the most prevailing sub-sins of hiring:

- The Panic Hire - you allowed the sin of fear to take over, and you hired the first person who came in and applied for the job.
- Handcuffed management - This one again is usually associated with the sin of fear. The staff runs the restaurant and usually not very well.

Sometimes it's important to remember that it's not the person you fail to hire that destroys your restaurant; it's a person you fail to fire.

Yes, running a restaurant is relatively easy. It's the people puzzle that makes it complex, with all of the emotions and psychological biases that humans carry inside their brains, creating a fascinating puzzle.

In short, it's people that make a restaurant work.

Where Have Restaurant Profits Gone?

If you listen to the news, you know that the restaurant industry continues to grow. Bruce Grindy, NRA Chief Economist, says in this post: "Restaurant job growth is projected to outpace the overall economy in 2016, and the industry will add more than 300,000 jobs for the sixth consecutive calendar year." That's awesome news!

However, restaurant profit margins seem to be shrinking and shrinking and shrinking.

So why do so many restaurants struggle? If things are so great and business is booming, why are so many not making the profits they should?

It's rather simple: bad planning.

The restaurant industry has a unique duality. On the one hand, it is a business of emotions. Passion, service, hospitality, pleasure, indulgence, and entertainment are common emotional drivers. It's also, however, a business of control. Inventory, systems, attention to detail, precision, and consistency are all needed to make a restaurant last. These two elements are much like yin and yang. They need each other to survive. The problems come when you focus too much on one and not the other.

Here are four common areas that will eat away at your restaurant's profits. Improve them to improve your restaurant's profit margin.

1. BAD PRICING STRATEGY

When you match other restaurants as far as menu items and then try to lower your pricing to undercut theirs, you lose. Your restaurant is now a commodity. You might get business in the short term, but those quick sales are not so great when you look at the bottom line.

You don't want to compete on price. You want to stand out on value.
So how do you do that?

1. Train your team to deliver better service. Invest in programs, books, even audio that make your people better. Remember: restaurants become better when the people in them become better.
2. Develop signature menu items. You need to be able to answer this question: Why do I drive to your restaurant? If you don't stand out in the market, you are blending in.
3. Don't get lured into a price war with other restaurants. Sometimes ego gets thrown in the pricing game, as competitors would rather sell something cheaper to take away guests from another restaurant. This will kill your restaurant›s profit margin.

2. BAD DELEGATION

Many restaurant owners have big visions for their business. Many restaurant owners get stuck working in their business instead of on their business. It's easy to get drawn in and be trapped there. You want your business to be successful, that's understandable. The problem is that most are doing work that they could easily delegate to other employees.

> *"Many restaurant owners get stuck working in their business instead of on their business."*

It's as simple as this: Your business will not grow until you focus on the things that can grow your business. Is your time being used wisely, sitting in the office writing schedules (something a manager could do), or would it be better spent networking and making sure your restaurant is at the top of people's minds? Are you spending your time wisely running to the store to buy products or training your team on how to manage their inventory better? Are these activities improving your restaurant profit margin?

3. BAD HIRING

We know that getting the right people on your team is important. Who you allow to interact with your guests is one of the critical decisions an owner or manager makes. Sometimes, it›s not the person you hire that hurts your restaurant... it›s the one you *don›t* fire.

Bad employees are a major reason your profits are not there. They don't care, and they waste products. They don't care, and they alienate your guests. They don't care, and they piss off the good employees who have to do the extra work they don't do. They clock in early and clock out late to ride the time clock and raise your labor costs. They throw away silverware because they're too lazy to retrieve it when it accidentally falls into the trash. These people are *stealing* from you in a way that is far worse than taking product. They steal your time and energy and drive good customers and other employees away. They are kissing your restaurant profit margin goodbye.

Avoid these hires at all costs, and remove them from your staff if you discover them.

4. BAD CONTROLS

Most restaurant owners know what they should do. They should cost out their menu. They should create a yearly marketing calendar. They should fix the chairs with rips in them. They should have a budget and a P&L. They should follow their restaurant business plan.

... They just should all over the place.

I know I have mentioned this a few times throughout the book. If you know there is something you should do in your restaurant to improve your bottom line, and you are not, then you need to turn that should into a must! Drop the excuses as to why you cannot get those things done. You don't have the right people? Hire the right people! You don't have time? Make time. You don't know how? Hire someone with knowledge. *We can do this all day....*

The reason your restaurant is not making the profits you want is the story you keep telling yourself about why you can't achieve your goals. Divorce the story and marry the truth.

You're going to need to make a real commitment to getting the restaurant profit margin you want — a real commitment. Talk is cheap. Actions and results are the only measures that matter.

Restaurant Profit Margin - 100% All or Nothing

In 1519, Hernando Cortez decided he wanted the treasures the Aztecs had, so he took 500 soldiers, 100 sailors, and 11 ships to the shores of the Yucatan. Cortez knew his men were outnumbered. He also knew that, in 600 years, no one had been able to conquer the Aztecs. Some of his men were unsure of their chance of success. Some even tried to seize some ships and head for Cuba. Cortez found out about this and wanted to make sure that his men were committed to the plan to take over the Aztec empire, so he ordered his men to burn the boats. Now that is going in with a 100% all or nothing mindset!

Too many restaurant owners operate with a noncommittal attitude. Your restaurant will never see the profits you want until you commit to doing whatever it takes to succeed. When failure is an option, there is a lack of commitment. Change is hard. The restaurant business can be a challenge. Get a mentor, a coach, or an advisor. Do something that puts you back in control of your restaurant. Develop a pricing strategy that sets you up as a brand leader, not a commodity. Delegate tasks that take you away from building your business. Get rid of those bad employees cutting into your profits. Stop making excuses and start making solutions.

Oh, and burn the fucking boats.

A Restaurant Coach™ Tip: Bad Days

If you are having a bad day (*yes, they do happen from time to time*), remember this:

If You Can't Change it, Then Change Your Attitude.

Sure, a co-worker might be a jerk to you.
Guests might be unreasonable.
Things don't always go your way. There will be things that pop up that are just bad timing.
However, your reactions to those things?
That's all on you.

If you find yourself starting to react and not respond (we'll talk about this more on your coaching call if we haven't already), here's my 3 Step Process:

1. **Call a time out.** You are allowed to take time to gather your thoughts and shift your thinking from reactionary (lizard brain or Limbic System) to the more rational part (the Neocortex). Just say, «With respect, I need 3 minutes to pause & process this.»

2. **Step away from the situation.** There is something about moving away from the scene that allows your brain to cool down faster from the «fight or flight» tone it's in.

3. **Breathe.** Yes. Take three deep breaths. Breathe deep and fill up your lungs. Then slowly exhale until all the air is released. Do this at least two more times. Also, you can say something to break your state (another topic talked about in coaching calls), here's one I use, and after saying it a few times I always find my state changes (it makes me laugh). When I breathe in I say, " In with anger (frustration or whatever you are feeling)." Then when I breathe out I say, "Out with love." I imagine my body is a filter that purges the bad energy and when I breathe out its good vibes.

You can either be a victim of circumstances and let them control you OR you can take control of your emotions. The choice (like so many others) is in your power.

SABOTAGING YOUR SUCCESS?

Things are going great for your restaurant. Then something bad happens. Maybe a one-star review on Yelp. Then your chef walks out. Then another thing. And another. Now you're stuck. It seems like no matter what you do, and you cannot seem to get out of this funk. You are in quicksand, and the more you fight, the more you sink.

Don't worry. This, too, shall pass. It's a quite common scenario. The main reasons this happens are:

1.   You have the wrong mindset.
2.   You are focused on the wrong things.

Mindset is Everything

Here is a simple question: Do you expect to be successful, or do you hope to be successful?

Knowing and hoping are two different mindsets. Having confidence (and knowing) is a strong emotion that can help carry you through troubled times. Hope is more like a beggar.

In 1964, Victor H. Vroom from the Yale School of Management studied the motivations behind decision-making and came up with what is known as Expectancy Theory. Expectancy is the belief that one's efforts will result in the attainment of the desired goal.

To better understand this theory, we must take into account the three components.

1. Self-efficacy: Remember the question above. Do you expect to be successful, or do you hope to be successful? Winners expect to reach their goal.
2. Goal difficulty: When goals are set too high, or performance expectations are too challenging, this will lead to low expectations.
3. Perceived control: This variable was brought to light back in the 1950s by Julian Rotter in a theory called Locus of Control. If you have an internal locus of control, you believe that you influence events and outcomes. On the other hand, if you have an external locus of control, you blame outside forces for everything that happens.

So how do you get out of the rut of a poor mindset? It takes time, energy, and effort to rise above a negative situation. So be patient. Set yourself up for small successes. In the war with your subconscious, it's better to win the small battles, then try to banish negativity in a single assault.

Set Yourself Up to Win

Play to Your Strengths. You will only excel when you play to your natural strengths. If you do not like spreadsheets and accounting, doing them yourself is a poor use of your strengths. Besides, if you're not very good at it, what are the chances that the information is correct? This is for the restaurant owner who thinks they know how to cost out their menu and come up with a theoretical cost of 21% when after further analysis reveals a food cost more toward the 42% mark.

Running a restaurant is a lot like playing chess. Each piece in the game has its strengths. Your job is to move each piece into a position where its natural strengths can become an asset.

Enter the Mentor. If the owner and manager influence the staff and the staff influences the guest experience, who influences the owner and manager? Enter the mentor.

Even ultra-successful entrepreneurs like Facebook's Mark Zuckerberg have used a mentor (he was Steve Jobs). Mentorship allows you to tap into the experience of another beyond your restaurant. Einstein was famous for saying that a problem cannot be solved on the level it was created. It's true.

Sometimes having a mentor can give you fresh eyes through which to look at a problem.

What You Focus on Becomes Reality. No, this is not praising the book, The Secret. However, it is true that where you place your focus, your energy will follow. Ever read an article about work-life balance? Well, that's a myth! If you work in the restaurant industry, it's like the elusive creature Bigfoot. We all want to believe it's real.

Life is never really in balance. When you focus on an area, things tend to improve in that area. Focus on your relationship, and it tends to become better. Focus on marketing, and sales tend to increase. The real trick is to balance the time you focus on each area. That's the real balance. They say time is money. No, money is money. The real currency with time is where you place your attention. In today's hyper-distracted world, those who can control their focus have real power.

Manage Your Calendar. Open your calendar. Most people have a few appointments there, and that's about it. Your calendar is probably one of the most underutilized focus tools you have available. All that blank area between appointments is called white space. For the ultra-productive and successful, white space is the enemy.

If you do not control your time and focus, someone else will control it for you. You need to schedule as much as you can into your calendar. The gym, social media time, date nights, training with staff, lunch service, pre-shift, dinner service, marketing, R&D... everything. Use your calendar as the gatekeeper of your time.

The best tip to avoid becoming overwhelmed and over-committed is learning this one simple word: no. If you had a very important business meeting on Tuesday at 3 p.m. and someone else asked to meet with you at that same time, you would have no problem telling them you had another obligation. Use that same mindset for every appointment on your calendar. If you schedule 45 minutes to work on marketing for your business, don't blow it off or cancel it. Treat each appointment on your calendar with the mindset that it's the most important business meeting you will attend.

Be a Real Leader. Sometimes you need to know that *you are the chokehold on your business growth*. Culture does flow from the owners/leaders down to the team. Your attitude and behavior have a direct impact on your team. It's a cycle known as The Betari Box.

It shows a correlation of how attitude and behavior go hand in hand. Our behavior is a mirror of our attitudes, which, in turn, affect the behavior of others. It becomes a circle of cause and effect. The way you act (your attitude) affects your behavior, which has an impact on others' attitudes, which has an impact on their behavior, which has an impact on your attitude.

The Betari Box

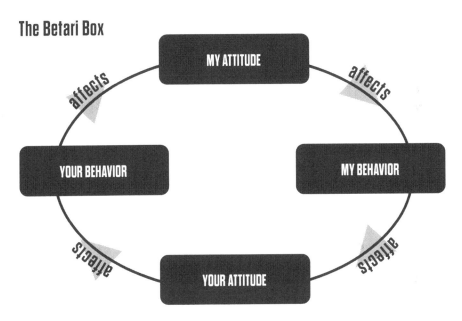

So how do you stop the circle? Quite simply, make sure your attitude is in check. If you think having little nicknames for your team is not affecting performance, you're wrong. Even if you don't tell them to their face the name you have for them, it has an impact on your attitude. That attitude will come through in your behavior and your nonverbal communication (which is 55%).

Being a real leader is about being a professional. That means your thoughts and actions act as one. Being in congruency with your core values and acting with integrity are non-negotiable leadership characteristics. Leadership is not something you can fake. Real leaders channel inner strength and confidence that come through in their actions.

Remember this: Talent and skill can take you to the top; however, it's your character and mindset that keeps you there.

The 12 Bullshit Lies You Tell Yourself That Hold Your Restaurant Hostage

I'm sure that the catchy title got your attention! You might be saying to yourself right now:

Bullshit lies? Who me?
Yes, you!

Now don't take it too personally because we all lie to ourselves from time to time. *Yes, even I've done it too, so welcome to the club!* When you admit it and don't let it control you, you can finally do something about it, and that's exactly why you and I are here! **I'm not going to give you a pass on your bullshit, I'm here to help you deal with your bullshit.** What's amazing is that in only one paragraph I have been able to say the word bullshit now five times (including the title)! Boom!

Hold onto something because this is going to get a little rough.

You and I are similar in the sense that we have been telling ourselves lies for years. I know I did, and if you're honest with yourself, you know you have as well. The first thing to do is to admit it. The second thing to do is to forgive yourself. The third thing to do is **stop it**.

If you read my books, blogs, or listen to my podcast, you've most likely heard me say this before *(if you are one of my private restaurant coaching clients, you hear this a lot!)* ...**awareness precedes choice and choice precedes change.** You first must be aware of it to change it! It only takes one letter to go from **chance to change**!

Lie #1: I don't have time.

Did you know that 26% of people think they don't have enough time?

What happened?

Did someone take your time?

No! You have the same 24 hours as everyone else in the world. So what's the logic behind this lie? You don't want to admit that you don't manage your time effectively. That's the real issue here. You went on a time shopping spree just giving it out like free lollipops at the bank, and now you have none left for the important things.

Stop wasting time by throwing it away at things that do not move your life or your restaurant forward! You are usually caught up in one or two of the four dimensions of time: mostly either distraction or demand. You're avoiding the tough stuff and doing the easy things that require very little energy (distraction). Or you're saying yes to everyone about everything, and you are running around at the demand (command) of others. There is nothing wrong with doing things for others as long as you also block off time for yourself. Psychologists call this having "healthy boundaries." Others might call this "growing a pair." You must always save time to move YOUR life forward while helping others.

This starts with understanding that time is not money. Money is money. You can always make more money. Sorry to break the bad news to you, however, you cannot stretch 24 hours into 25.

Lie #2: There are no good people out there to hire.

If this lie were true, then no restaurants would exist. There are amazing people out there working in restaurants every single day. It might be that you've become a little jaded dealing with some of the less than desirable employees. Okay, here comes the gut punch: you hired them!

Poor hiring decisions are the number one cause of having bad staff on your team. Desperation does not mean you lower your standards to fill a slot on the schedule! This is commonly referred to as "panic hiring," and it causes more problems than you think.

Not only do you allow a toxic and poor performer into your culture, you allow them to spread their negativity and infect the others on your team. A virus doesn't kill you at first. It slowly infiltrates the system and then depletes the healthy cells. What it leaves behind is a hollow shell of what was once great!

The best defense is to have high standards for who is a great match for your culture. Know your core values and ask new candidates what values they have. Stop hiring for experience and instead focus more on personality. You can train skills (if they are trainable and coachable), you cannot change personality easily (even though most think they can).

Lie #3: I can't do that.

Okay, this is a lie you say when you should be saying, **"I won't do that."** It's always better, to be honest. If you don't want to do something, please don't say yes and then do a half-ass job! That is probably the greatest sin out there.... succumbing to mediocre performance due to poor commitment.

Can't and won't say something under the surface that you might not realize. Can't says it's not in your control or power. Won't says it goes against your core values and moral compass. Which one would a confident person use? I won't always tips the power scale in your favor. You stood up for something you believe in. The world needs more people that are willing to stand up for what they believe in.

Lie #4: I'm working hard.

Why is it that we think hard work is what life is all about? Here is a big truth bomb coming your way: *you are not rewarded for hard work; you are rewarded for results.*

Hey, if you are working long hours for extended periods you are either in one of two spots:

You suck at time management.

Or

You suck at hiring, training, and leading people.

I get it that working long hours is required for startup restaurants or taking over a new team. If it's a year down the road and you are still working crazy hours, then you, my friend, are addicted to the drama, and you need an intervention!

Your self-worth had become dependent on how much your team needs you. Your job should always be to replace yourself. Remember that if you can't be replaced, you can't be promoted. That also holds true for restaurant brands that want to expand to multiple locations. Running one to two restaurants is fairly easy. Once you get past three you cannot run that many restaurants with the same mindset that you did when you were smaller.

I don't care if you work 80 hours a week or 40! It all comes down to these questions:

Are you getting results?
Are you growing yourself?
Are you growing your brand?
Are you growing your team?

The number of hours you put in or the whining that you work so hard is just a cry for attention. Stop it. Drama is great for movies and bad for restaurants! The drama starts and stops with the leader of the restaurant. What you tolerate you get!

Don't tell me how hard you work. Tell me what the hell you got done this week to move your life and your restaurant forward? Until you can be honest with yourself, you are just wasting time looking for attention. Losers want attention. Winners want results!

Lie #5: It is what it is.

The saying, "It is what it is." is such bullshit. It's exactly what you accept it to be. If you're fine with mediocrity, then admit it; just don't give it an excuse that "it is what it is."

I always say that if you want a better life or restaurant, then you ask better quality questions! It is what it is, is such a cop-out that drifts straight towards mediocrity.

What are you going to do about it?
What are you prepared to do to change shit?
What the fuck do you want from this?
What is your outcome?

Answer those questions the next time you reach for that easy out of "it is what it is," and you'll see your life dramatically change for the better.

Remember that excuses beget excuses.

Lie #6: That won't happen to me.

Denial is a powerful drug. Probably more than all opioids combined. Why? Because it robs you of a better future. Denial steals away your opportunity to improve. It leaves you in a state called learned helplessness. You're just there thinking that it won't happen to you.

A lot of restaurants are going to close this year, and that is a fact of the economy. Don't say it can't happen to you. You are a business like any other, and they all have a risk of going out of business! Markets change rapidly sometimes. If you are in denial that it won't happen to you...it's a pretty good bet that it WILL happen to you!

Denial is usually followed around by its cousin called Foolish Pride. The next to visit is called Failure. I'm sure that the dozen or so restaurants that closed last month never thought it would happen to them too. Many probably could have been saved if they would have asked for help.

I run into a restaurant in trouble way more than I do ones that are performing at their potential. This is a sad situation that used to bother me. Why would someone who is running their restaurant into the ground not reach out and grab the life preserver being offered to them? That damn foolish pride they have. They would rather go down with the sinking ship.

I can't help a restaurant unless they are willing to do three things:

1. **You must listen.** I usually start this conversation with the question, "Do you know the difference between advice and opinion?". Everyone has an opinion about how to run your restaurant. Advice is from a

professional who has been there and is pretty much telling you this is the course of action you must take now. I only give advice.

2. **You must take action.** Your lack of taking action and getting the right things done is what got you in this situation. When I give you a deadline, you better have a real fucking awesome reason why you didn't get it done, or we won't be working together much longer. I am hired to get you the restaurant and life you want! You can be mediocre without me.

3. **You must be patient.** It took you some time to get into this mess you are in, and it takes about half of that amount of time to get you rewired for success. So if you've been running amuck for two years, expect at least a year to get your shit together. Oh, and that's if you follow rules one and two above.

A lot of restaurants come to me, asking for coaching. They say they want to change. They say they want to maximize profits. They say they want to dominate their market. They say they want a business that doesn't consume their personal life. So, they start my program. Within a month most have some bullshit excuse why they need to stop.

Be sure you want it because I am dedicated to getting it for you, but you're going to need to put in the work. I will work as hard as you for your brand. I won't work harder than you for your brand. *Show me you want it, and I'll give it to you.*

Lie #7: I can change that person.

Here comes another lie that is disguised in the shape of denial. **Consider for a moment how hard it is to change yourself, and you'll finally see what little chance you have of changing other people.**

Here's the other thing about this that you might not realize...most people are comfortable with where they are! The comfort zone is full of lazy and uninspired people who are more like zombies living a life of mediocrity. Granted, they complain all the time and point fingers at who is to blame for the shit life they have (they never point the blame at themselves by the way). Yet, they don't do anything to improve their situation. Here's some harsh reality: if you don't care enough to change your life. It will never happen.

So, thinking that you are going to change someone else who doesn't want to change is like saying you are going to turn day into night just because you think it would be better for the day. It's not going to happen.

Before you go on a crusade to change someone, you need to ask yourself if they want to be changed?

If you truly want to have an impact on the people around you, then change yourself first. Be the example and set the standard. People are more likely to change when they see someone who inspires them. All improvement starts with self-improvement.

Lie #8: I don't judge people.

Please excuse me while I clear my throat...*bullshit!*

You, me, and everyone else in the world does judge people to some extent. I don't care how holy or self-righteous you think you are. We all, at our fundamental core, are hypocrites. We wear a mask of who we want the world to see. We pretend that we're great when inside we suffer. We smile when we want to scream to the heavens. We laugh when we want to cry. I've done it too so don't think you're alone.

Breaking free from this is when you decide you have nothing to prove to others. You only need to be honest and true to yourself. That starts with a little core value called integrity. You see, once we sell out our moral compass, it's easy to be swayed into more compromise. It's easier to lie and deceive yourself. That voice in your head talking shit is just keeping you from being authentic. It's suppression of your soul.

Why do we judge others? It's quite simple: our ego, greed, and envy control us. They make us jealous and judgmental of others. We fear and throw shade at the things that we feel threaten us. Fear is the mind-killer. It prays on that weak part of your subconscious that is always looking to protect you from...well, everything! You can thank our primal ancestors for that. Granted, it served the human race for millions of years, and it keeps us safe from predators that wanted to have us for dinner. Now, it tends to be stopping most from getting the restaurant and life they desire.

Let's be clear on something: danger is real; fear is a choice.

Lie #9: I'll do it tomorrow.

The fallacy of foresight! We always believe that the promise of tomorrow is going to save us. Well, what if tomorrow doesn't come? Ever think about that? Most likely, you don't think about it too often (or until someone you know passes away unexpectedly). That mortality thing is a real bitch. Let me tell you from first-hand experience that death will come for you one day. Maybe, if you're really lucky you might get another chance at life (like I did when I had a cardiac arrest in September 2018).

Death changes your outlook pretty dramatically and very quickly. I realized that there were a lot of things I had still to do, and I wanted to leave a dent in the industry (Yes, I said a dent! Everyone wants to have an impact! How average is that?). Getting a second chance was a harsh wake-up call for me. I would offer this up as a wakeup call to you as well before your time is up. Whatever you want to do, make a plan and fucking do it! Do it now!

Get your calendar out and start to schedule as much as you can for each day. You must start living each day knowing that the clock is ticking, and you do not get unlimited time. Time is the one thing in the entire universe that doesn't discriminate. It doesn't care where you live, what religion you are, what race you are...it keeps ticking away. We all have the same 24 hours each day. The difference between those that get the life they want is how they use those 24 hours. Are you investing them to become better or wasting them in distraction doing activities that do not have any return on your investment? Stop playing small and stop wasting time. Trust me that you don't have any to spare.

Lie #10: If I can get (insert anything), then I'll be happy.

The quest for material things is driven by the ego. Take it from a guy who has had the good things in life that they don't make you happy for very long. Sure, the high-end sports car is fun to drive until it has maintenance issues. They pool in the backyard will impress your friends until you have to clean up the puke from the party. The supermodel looking partner is fun until you try to have an intelligent conversation with them.

Stop chasing after things that don't contribute to long term happiness. What does? Becoming a better human being! Start being compassionate. Teach or mentor someone. Volunteer at a food bank. Donate some of those clothes you are never going to wear again to a shelter. Spend some time out in nature, just appreciating how amazing the world is. Share a sunset or watch the stars with someone you love.

I'm not saying to become a monk and forsaken all material possessions. I'm saying don't make them the end all, be all things you think will make you happy. Start being happy now.

Here's a little secret to success: be happy with who you are. Love what you do. Make it your mission to serve others and improve their lives, and you will find the money, and the rewards come to you. We chase the wrong things. Stop chasing the stuff and start filling your heart with service to others.

Lie #11: I'm just not lucky.

Here's the thing about the universe and energy...once you declare it, the universe works to make sure you get it! Call it a self-filling prophecy. You truly get what you focus on.

If you say you are not lucky, we'll guess what? You will find that Lady Luck tends to stay away from you. Say you suck at love, and your love life will suck. Declare that your staff is a bunch of idiots, and you'll see you are surrounded by them. The words you regularly use (habit) become the experience you speak of.

Now, this doesn't mean that if you start saying positive things tomorrow, that all is going to be right with your world in a few days. You're going to have to back your words up with a little thing called belief. You can say it all you want, and if you don't believe it deep down inside, then it won't materialize.

If you declare it, share it, believe it, and take action towards it, then I can say with confidence that you will most likely get it. I have been down this road many times, and unlike the bullshit propagated in the hot book The Secret, you can't wish it to happen. You are going to need to move towards it too!

Watch the words and things you say because they form your reality. #truestory

Lie #12: If I want anything done right, I have to do it myself.

Woe is me! You poor thing, doing all the work. Let's clear the air on this major bullshit. You don't trust your team and refuse to give up control. That is why you do most of the work! You have turned your team into a bunch of dependent workers who are afraid of their shadow because you didn't train them or allowed them to make mistakes.

Please don't give me the perfectionist crap either. You're not a perfectionist; you're just a weak leader that is so in denial that you can't help anyone let alone yourself. Need creates more need. When you have a team that is not empowered to make mistakes and learn, you have a crew that hovers at mediocrity. They never get better. They never search for growth. You're just stuck with them in a perpetual Groundhog Day, living the same day over and over again.

Stop treating your team like they are incompetent. They're not. You keep them held down in learned helplessness and then whine and complain about all the work you do. Stop it because, honestly, no one cares how many hours you put in or how hard you say you work. You are committing the biggest lie of all...you are lying to yourself.

Without trust, relationships die. Without mistakes, there is no growth. Without opportunity, people leave. Stop trying to carry the entire restaurant on your back. Share some of the responsibilities. Share some of the tasks that you are not good at. Share some of the glory. Create a culture where it's more "we" than "me." You don't have to do it all yourself unless you choose to. Remember that you always have a choice.

Now maybe you'll reflect on this list and, finally, take some actions to change yourself. If you read this far, my prediction would be that you will start to make some changes. Here's the thing, be easy on yourself and give yourself a little break. By showing up every day with a new attitude you will start to see some changes. It's not the big bold changes that have the deepest impact on your life. It's the small everyday consistent changes that do.

Start small. Be steady. Commit. Stay the course. Adjust your habits to get the results you want. *Become obsessed with becoming a better version of yourself.*

TRENDS

"Don't follow trends, start trends!"

-Frank Capra

Online Review Obsession and Why It's Killing You

Online review sites. We love them when they are kind, and we loathe them when they say less than flattering things about our restaurant. Research at Harvard has shown that reviews can have an impact on your sales. Get another star and boom; sales can increase 5 to 9%. It's easy to see why we crave positive online reviews. The problem comes when we become obsessed with them.

Obsession is a dual-edged sword that can truly cut both ways. When you are driven and obsessed with improving every single day or what the Japanese call Kaizen, it's a philosophy of constant and never-ending improvement that can set your restaurant up for long term success. In fact, in today's market you need to have a little Kaizen in your core values and mission. If you are not improving, then you are standing still. It's not a good thing to stand still while your competitors are innovating, improving, and creating strategic plans to take your market share. Being obsessed is good when it pushes you to want to do more and be more. This is internal obsession. You want more of this.

The other side of the obsession sword is when we are so focused on what others are doing and what they have. This obsession stems from primal emotions of greed, envy, and jealousy. These emotions pull your attention away from your restaurant and what you can control, to others, and what they are doing. Of course, you want to be aware of what is going on in your market. Contrary to popular belief ignorance is not bliss if you run a restaurant. Ignorance is just ignorance. Obsession takes an ugly turn when it consumes our focus and energy. This is external obsession. You do not want this.

To help control the external obsession monster from taking you over, here are a couple of things you need to consider:

1. 20% OF ONLINE REVIEWS ARE FAKE.

A problem started when Harvard put out that report stating that a one-star increase was good for a 9% increase in sales. It started an online "gold rush" of less than reputable restaurant owners flooding online review sites with fake reviews, both good and bad.

They pumped up their brand with good reviews and went around bashing their competition with negative reviews. These types of individuals are the ones who bring discredit to our industry. Their marketing campaigns (if you could even call them that) are more like ones you would see running for President of the United States...it turns into a negativity media storm. That is a storm you want to avoid.

2. OF COURSE, YOU ARE GOING TO GET SOME BAD REVIEWS

You cannot make everyone happy when you get a bad review (and it will happen). You need to stop and ask yourself a question: *Is it true?*

If you can say with 100% assurance that it is not true, then take it for what it is...a personal opinion. Everyone is entitled to their opinion. That is what makes this country great.

Now, if there is some truth behind it, then you have you be honest with yourself that all might not be perfect in your restaurant. That requires getting a big glass of water and swallowing three pills called ego, pride, and denial. One or all of those three are usually the reasons that keep restaurant owners and operators stuck. Choke them down, and you are on your way to the restaurant you know it can become.

Taking accountability is freeing and necessary for your brand to grow and survive. Here are some questions to ask if you do find yourself faced with a bad review that could be true:

- *Did you have clear standards that are set in stone like It was carved in a tablet as a commandment?*
- *Do you have a written list of core values that lead the team with their actions? Do you talk about your core values every day to your team?*
- *Are you committed to training every single day? Do you train, teach, and develop your team daily?*

If you are honest, then you might see some opportunities there that you need to work on. Even if you answered "yes" to all of those questions, then ask yourself: "Could you take it to the next level? Could you do more and become even better?" If you said "no" to those questions, please go back to getting that glass of water and swallowing the three pills mentioned before.

Now if you do get a bad review, there are some steps to take:

A. Apologize for not meeting expectations. This is a great way to declare that you are compassionate to the guest. Say something along the lines of: "I am truly sorry we did not meet your expectations that is not the experience we work towards."

B. Ask for a chance to earn their business back. Most people will give you another chance if you ask for it. However, the request must be within 24 hours of the bad review. Remember that people go online to complain because they felt the situation was not resolved while at the restaurant.

The longer time you take to respond (*notice the word respond not react*), the harder it will be to rebuild trust. See that is what happens in a bad review.... *there is a breakdown of trust between the guest and your brand.* When you break a brand promise you'll find it hard to recover especially if you avoid it. Ask Chipotle about the damage breaking trust with the guests can have.

Say something like: "I would like the opportunity to earn your business again and show you the true [INSERT YOUR RESTAURANT HERE] experience. My name is [YOUR NAME HERE], and please ask for me when you come in so I can personally come by and say thank you for the chance to make this right."

C. Avoid excuses. The last thing you want to do is start throwing out excuses as to why you dropped the ball. Remember that the purpose of responding to bad online reviews is to rebuild trust and get the guest to come back. Not throwing out excuses or arguing with the guest in an online format. "Well, we were short-staffed and did the best we could" or "You ate over half of the steak before you complained about it!" Here's a favorite I have seen, "No one on our staff even has the hair color of the one you found in your food." Yipes!

D. Always write a draft in another app and have another person read it. This extra step or two can save you from lashing out in a reactive state and not responding professionally. Just look at those you hear about that sent out a tweet and then delete it however not before others have taken screenshots of it that now become a meme floating around the internet. Becoming a meme is not a good idea.

Remember that word-of-mouth has become "world-of-mouth" with a click of a button. Have you heard of Amy's Baking Company in Scottsdale, Arizona? They appeared a few years back on an episode of Kitchen Nightmares with Chef Gordon Ramsey, and it was the first time that the chef had to walk away. The couple who owned the restaurant were infamous for arguing with guests online and letting it escalate to some crazy levels. The business is now closed.

Where Focus Goes, Energy Flows

This is a great maxim to write down and place it where it can be a constant reminder to you. Where focus goes, energy flows. Meaning where you place your focus is where you will see results. It's not rocket science. What you pay attention to will get better *if you put some action behind it*. The problem with external obsession is that you are taking your focus away from your business. Now, being aware of your market is important. When your time, energy and focus become obsessed with what others are doing, how many cars are in their parking lot, and all the likes they get on Facebook…then you have a problem. *Being informed is great. Being obsessed is not.*

Internal obsession is the key to maximizing your resources. You need to tap into your strengths and those of the team to become outstanding in a crowded market. Now, if becoming outstanding were easy, we would not have the epidemic of average restaurants that we do.

Sadly, average is the new standard in the restaurant industry. Average is a failing formula for long term success. Most restaurants that seek out a business coach are either in a place of desperation or inspiration. Desperate restaurants are struggling, and they are looking for someone to get them back on track quickly. The inspired restaurants are doing great and have an internal drive and know that they could do even more and expand their brand.

The restaurants in the middle who are average never reach out to become better because they are comfortable. Being comfortable is just complacency, and being complacent is slow death to a restaurant. It's like they are floating down the river happy and carefree. Then, they notice up ahead is Niagara Falls and their brand is about to go over the edge. Very few can change direction and paddle fast enough to avoid going over the falls. Having a coach or mentor helps you look ahead and create a strategic plan for long term success. They also can help you break free from unhealthy obsessions that are hurting your business. Online reviews are one obsession that can hurt your restaurant when that obsession turns and consumes your focus. Start by re-channeling that by asking yourself better questions like:

- *What can you do to improve your menu?*
- *What can you do to make your service stand out in the market?*
- *What can you do to become a better leader?*
- *What can you do to make your team better?*

These are the questions you want to put your time, energy, and focus into. These are the questions that build better restaurants.

Control your obsessions, or they will control you.

The Slow Death of Restaurants

Whether you want to admit it or not, there is a storm coming. It's not going to be good for a lot of budding restauranteurs who think that the lure of fame and fortune await them in the restaurant business.

In 2016, for example, there were 620,807 restaurants across the country, down 1.6 percent compared with a year ago. That's the largest decrease since 1998. That decline amounts to about 9,998 restaurant closures year over year, and most of them were independent restaurants. The overall count included 221,810 full-service independent restaurants in fall 2016, marking a decline of 3.7 percent year over year for that segment specifically. That translates to a loss of 9,784 independent restaurants.

For smart operators that have their act together, this is a perfect opportunity to rise above as an economic survival of the fittest will see the closure of more restaurants in the next two years than ever before. The restaurant bubble is about to burst, and you'll want to make sure your brand is ready for the storm. Only the strong will survive.

So how did we get here? What brought about this devolution of the industry?

No Experience Needed

Have you got a checkbook? Then you can open a restaurant. There are few industries that have no qualifications for entry quite like the restaurant business. Anyone can open a restaurant with nothing more than a bankroll. Opening a restaurant is not the hard part. Making money at it is a challenge.

The problem is that while some might have a brilliant idea for a concept, they never set themselves up for long term success. You need systems and a solid business strategy to make it in the uber-competitive market today. Having good food and good service is the standard everyone expects good. Even fast-food concepts provide "good." That's the problem. Those chains have lowered the threshold on what the modern guest expects. We have become desensitized to what "good" really is anymore.

Good enough is not very good today. It's average. Being average is a recipe for failure. Okay, let's be honest here...being average sucks. Even if you make enough to break even or by chance, make a profit one or two months, your business will never thrive. It's like most restaurants are in a coma, and the only reason no one pulls the plug is that they still cling to hope. Hope is not a strategy for running a restaurant.

Outdated Management

The way most run their restaurants today is very similar to how they have been run for the last 20 years. Sure, we might have new technology that allows us to schedule our team online, cool programs that let us order food without calling a sales rep, and even amazing POS systems that can tell us who our top guests are and how much they spend on average.

However, we still treat people the same way.

We have the technology, yet we talk **down** to the team instead of **to** the team. We order online and get upset that our vendor stopped "servicing" our account. We know more about our guests than ever before, yet we don't engage with them.

We use carrots and sticks to keep our team in line. We use management techniques and theories that need to be taken out back and buried. The workforce has evolved, and we as an industry have not. We fail to learn and update ourselves to deal with the millennials and the disruptive Gen Z. We are captains of a ship that has mutinied and left us talking to ourselves. We have lost touch with the people who work with us and blame them for the pain we experience.

You'll need to do better if you want to retain talent.

The Cult of Celebrity Chefs

The last 15 years have seen the rise and worship of the TV chef. Some celebrity chefs are great chefs and business leaders. What did The Food Network focus on when they launched?

Cooking.

Much like MTV that at one time played music videos, the Food Network became obsessed with ratings and trying to capture a bigger piece of the viewership. Along the way, they needed bigger and brasher shows, and before you knew it, the reality cooking show was born, and with it came visions of grandeur for young culinary sponges looking to be the next star chef.

The younger generation does not see the years' seasoned pros had to endure to rise to the top. Not that there is a lot of room at the top...hence why it is called "the top." This new generation has lost touch with the real "reality" of the industry because much of their view has been tainted by reality TV. Gordon Ramsey yells and calls people a "donkey," and that is what they think chefs do. Can chefs be ball busters? Yes. Can they also be compassionate mentors? Yes.

Bad Press

How can we combat bad press? Share the positive side of the industry. Stop posting about your food and specials and post about the human side. Show your team having fun. Show your guests having fun. Show yourself having fun.

Now there are a bunch of memes floating around the internet that poke fun at the business and really at heart perpetuate the deep troubles that plague our industry — Front-Of-The-House versus Back-Of-the-house. Granted, being a chef, I find them funny too. However, if I share them am I helping the industry or just keeping the negative energy and feeling alive? You can be funny and still not put down people. That's being creative and not being mean. Being mean is easy. Easy is not the way to build the bridge to future generations looking to make our business their business.

Many people love to talk about the war **FOR** talent. What we have is a war **WITH** talent. We think it's us against them. It's not. It's us against the other industries vying to capture the workforce to them. What do we need to do as an industry to attract the younger generation? Stop the negative mindset and press that is fueling the fire of how bad it is to work in a restaurant.

There is a storm coming. Are you and your restaurant ready for it? Will you survive? Only you know that answer. If you are hesitant and have doubts, then this would be a good time to find a mentor or business coach to help you prepare.

Just do something to make sure you're ready. You can sit back, keep doing the same things, and hope you'll get through the fallout. Then again, you know my feeling about relying on hope. If you refuse to take action and make a choice, a choice will be made for you.

Whatever you decide, be sure you are ready for the outcome.

5 Roadblocks Stopping You from Getting the Restaurant You Want

Step into the office and have a seat on the couch. Let's talk about what is going on in your restaurant. **Actually, let's talk about what's going on within your mind.**

The precipice of all business problems (at their foundation) are people problems. Those people problems are generally self-inflicted from the perceptions we carry around. **We can, at times be our own worst enemy.**

Don't feel bad about this. You're human, and part of that is understanding all the flaws that make us human. Every New Year, we make a long list of "resolutions" that we vow "this year," we are going to do! Then by the end of January we've fallen back into old routines and excuses why we couldn't make it happen. If you want to stop that madness, then pay attention to the following five psychological principles that get in your way from getting the restaurant and life you truly desire.

1. THE HABIT LOOP

Problem: You are a product of your habits. Most of them operate under the surface like an old operating system on your computer that keeps doing what it always has done for years. Even when you try to update your mental software, there it is running the same habits you have done for year after year.

You might say that it's just the way you are...**no**; *it's the way you choose to be*. If not, you would have taken steps to change that. Your habits are like a warm blanket that calls to you on a cold night. "Just stay here with me," it whispers. You stay and remain stuck on a never-ending habit loop. Cue (trigger), craving (want), response (habit), reward (result), repeat.

Now, if your habit is a bad one, it does not give you a positive result, and you stay stuck in the same loop over and over. It's like you're on a giant hamster wheel. You keep spinning in circles day after day with no real progress or change in your life or your restaurant.

Solution: You need to interrupt the habit loop at the point of response. The key is that the new response must be a positive one. Many people try each year to stop smoking. The problem is they substitute the reaching for a cigarette with a piece of candy. Soon, you find that the cigarette habit now had been replaced by a candy habit. We wonder why diabetes is an epidemic. You can't solve a bad habit with another bad habit.

2. IDENTITY

Problem: You are who you think you are. That may sound simplistic, yet it's very powerful in understanding most of your actions. You may have been born with some things that you did not choose, like family, race, and genetics. You do have a choice about how you show up in the world. That's your identity, and it controls you more than you think. Just look at a common identity; many can relate to political parties. On a basic level there are Republicans, and there are Democrats. You are not born one or the other. You choose to identify with one party or the other. Once you say that is who you are (your identity), you act in the way that you feel you should be in alignment with your identity. People can go to extremes to protect their identities. When you lose that you go through what psychologist call an identity crisis

Solution: Pick your identity carefully. *Very carefully.* Let's look at a common restaurant position, such as a manager versus a leader. What title you identify with plays a big part in your actions and behavior because it is your identity. A manager tends to "manage" the shift. They run from problem to problem putting out the fires. They use outdated management theories that "push" people to get results. A leader on the other hand truly steps out in front to lead their team. They elevate their team my being out in front and "pulling" the team in their direction through clear core values, respect, and appreciation.

3. COGNITIVE BIASES

Problem: Your brain is bombarded with millions of bits of information every single minute. There is so much coming into your senses simultaneously that you would not be able to handle it if it wasn't for some shortcuts you've developed from evolution. These problems solving shortcuts are called heuristics. Inside these shortcuts are a group of codes called cognitive biases. Think of these biases as a math formula. A + B = C.

Sometimes these shortcuts help us to survive. See bear + fear bear = run from the bear. Sometimes these can also hold us stuck into stinking thinking. Here are a few of the 104 cognitive biases (named by Wikipedia) that can help us and also hold us back:

- Confirmation Bias: we tend to look for evidence that supports our beliefs. If you walk into the restroom when you first arrive at a restaurant and if it's a total mess, your brain could easily conclude that the kitchen must be dirty too! Is it true? Most likely not. However, your biases start looking for evidence to support your new-found belief system. If you think there are no good people in the labor pool to hire, you'll tend to see the bad one that comes into apply. The old saying that seek and you shall find is dead-on accurate.

- Blind Spot Bias: failing to recognize your own cognitive biases is a bias itself. People tend to see the faults in others way more than they do in themselves.

- Planning Fallacy: The planning fallacy is a phenomenon in which predictions about how much time will be needed to complete a future task display an optimistic bias and underestimate the time needed. We tend to think we can get a project done far sooner than it takes!

Solution: Be open to the idea that your brain plays tricks on you. Being aware is always the first step to a better life. Awareness precedes choice, and choice precedes change. The best way to unravel a cognitive bias is to question it. Ask yourself a question that breaks your thinking patterns. An easy one is, "What would I have to believe for this to be true?" Or "What else could this mean?" Now the trick is you search for positive answers; don't be lured into the negative, gloom, and doom mindset. There is always a positive angle if you look for it. Sometimes you're just going to need to look hard for the positive!

4. LOCUS OF CONTROL

Problem: Here's the million-dollar question: Do you feel you control the outcomes in your life, or are you just at the whims of the universe? This at its essence is called the locus of control. If you have an external locus of control, you feel events are mostly out of your control, and life happens to you. When you have an internal locus of control you feel that the actions you take have an impact on your life.

Solution: If you truly want to get control of your life, it all starts here by taking control of your mindset! Stop the blame game and step up to the reality that you are in charge of how you respond to life events. Notice that last sentence mentioned the word "respond." Here is where the power of words comes into play. If you go to the doctor and they say you are having a "reaction" to the medication...that's bad. If they say you are "responding" to the medication...that's great! Each day when things happen you have a choice to either react or respond.

You will never control events, people, or the weather (*no matter how hard you try*). What you do control is how you interpret the events. To give you a clear understanding of this, let's explore a famous Shakespeare quote: *"Nothing is either good or bad, but thinking makes it so."*

Nothing has meaning until you attach one to it. If you react, you get emotional and lose control of your mindset. If you choose to respond, you have your mind under control.

The other way you can gain an internal locus of control is to change the meaning of the event. If nothing has meaning until you attach one to it, then changing the meaning will conversely change the way you look at it. Now, this is easy to see on the surface. It's a major challenge to implement it. Once again you have some bad habits up in the grey matter atop your body. Your brain and your habits like things the way they are, and they will put up a resistance. Deal with that and just be committed to making better choices.

5. MOTIVATION

Problem: You were probably told many times as a manager, you need to motivate your staff. Here's why that never quite works out the way you want. You're motivating them by what motivates you! Now if they share your goals, values, and personality then you might have a good connection, and your chances of motivating them are pretty good. People like people who are like themselves. The reality is that most people on your team are diverse and not motivated by the things that motivate you.

The other key thing to know is the difference between compliance and commitment. Compliance is the default mode of the average worker. They do just enough work to keep their job. They do things based on your reasons. Their heart isn't into their job, and most go through the motions. No heart. No passion. They are just working for that paycheck.

When you can get your team to find a reason that resonates with their values and it personal, then you get a commitment. Now they do things based on their reasons and not just yours. This leads us to see that true motivation is an inside job. Looking back at our compliance versus commitment discussion... what those two are in psychology speak is extrinsic motivation (compliance) and intrinsic motivation (commitment).

Solution: Stop trying to motivate others by what motivates you! This requires a technique that is not commonly practiced in average restaurants...you need to talk to your team. I never said it was rocket science! Motivation is more human science. You must talk to your team and dig down to find out what is important to them.

What are their short term and long term goals? What lights them up? Any hobbies? How about a crazy dream (goal) that they have? What's important to them?

These questions are essential to getting them to open up and talk to you. Now, fair warning...if you haven't had sit down conversations with your team, they will assume they are in trouble. Assure them that you want to get to know more about them. No need to freak people out for wanting to have a "get to know you better" talk. When your team does open up and talk to you, take notes! Now take that information and use it to help motivate your team. If someone values family, perhaps you could offer to host a party to celebrate their wedding anniversary? Your options and your world will open up when you open up to your team!

These psychological are not restricted to just your restaurant. All restaurants around the world have similar problems! People problems are the major reason restaurants struggle day in and day out. It's easy to point blame and say it's that person's fault. Your restaurant and your life will never (I mean never ever) improve until you step up and take total accountability for everything that happens in your restaurant and your personal life!

Is it easy? *Hell no.* It's going to be the fight of your life to overcome bad habits, connect with your true identity, be aware of those cognitive biases that limit you, develop your locus of control, and understand what motivates your team.

Will it be worth it all? *That would be a hell yes!*

Don't miss the opportunity to become the best version of yourself. To get there, you need a map!

Every destination needs a **M.A.P.** or what I like to think of as a **Massive Action Plan**! You need to know where you are and exactly where you want to go. Then you plot a course of action to get there. You cannot drive from LA to New York City in one day. You must make strategic stops along the way to hit your end goal.

What is the first thing you need to do to get you moving in the right direction? As you begin, **focus on the actions required and not the end result**. A small step is easier than a leap. Once the first step is made, it is easier to continue down the right path to your desired destination.

To help my clients maximize their potential, I have created a **signature coaching M.A.P.** that will get you from Mediocrity to the **Summit of Outstanding**!

The first step is to admit where you are in your journey. Many start in the land of average or what I refer to as **The Valley of Mediocrity**. Here you are pretty much surviving. Sales are up and down and so is your cash flow. The staff manages you more than you manage them. You are living a life of stress and overwhelm.

The most effective way to move out of the valley is to surround yourself with people that have a desire to succeed and are on a similar path. **The Restaurant Coach**™ **Nation** is the first stop. Here is a group of **Industry Sisters and Brothers** who are committed to getting the restaurant and life they desire. You see, there are others out there who want it all and this **Private Facebook Grou**p allows us to inspire and help each other. TRC Nation even has a **FREE 8-week Mentor Program** designed to help you get results and take that first big step to a better life.

If you are not a member yet, then head over to sign up. It's FREE; all you need to do is answer a couple of questions before getting access to the private group. If you are not accepted, most likely it's because you didn't answer the questions. *You see, that was test number one.* We want to have only people dedicated to following directions and committed to becoming better inside **TRC Nation.**

Head over to Facebook to join!

FINAL THOUGHTS

Client: I fear the new restaurant opening down the street.

Me: You need to fear mediocrity.

Donald Burns, The Restaurant Coach™

Easy is NOT an Option

Sometimes the best option is not the logical one. Pararescue teams train for combat search and rescue operations in a wide range of terrains and adverse conditions. Sometimes these include rather rugged and remote areas where parachuting into a nice, open, and clear field isn't an option.

One aspect of Pararescue training is doing parachute jumps in less than ideal scenarios. You might do a low attitude "hop-n-pop," a water jump while wearing full SCUBA gear, or the tree jump. Wait—would you want to hit a tree purposely?

Heavily forested areas are usually the terrain where civilians out for a weekend hike get into trouble. While the mission of Pararescue is primarily combat search and rescue, they also serve in a civilian capacity as well.

A middle-aged couple wanders off the trail to explore. One of them has a heart attack, and the other is helpless. The area is too densely populated with trees, and time is limited. Terrain and wind make a helicopter extraction too risky. What do you do? You'll need to jump in.

The Parachutist Rough Terrain System (nicknamed "the tree suit") is designed with padding and a special strap that designed to protect if you happen to wind up straddling a tree limb. In Pararescue School we tested this system by putting on the suit and letting others try to kick us in the nuts (perhaps not the smartest test but effective nonetheless). My teammate Bryon Kelly once tested this with me by taking two steps back, asking if I was ready, and pausing long enough for me to take a deep breath and nod "yes." He then kicked me like he was going for a 60-yard field goal in the Super Bowl. The kick picked me up off the ground (it felt like I was two feet in the air). The good news? The suit worked!

The suit is bulky as hell. It has a huge pocket on the side of one leg with a repelling rope inside. The ideal plan when you jump into heavily forested terrain is to avoid getting hung up in a tree (which you usually do). Once your chute is pretty much braided into the tree limbs, you take the rope out of the pocket and tie it through the parachute risers, then run the rope through a rescue carabiner for repelling, cut yourself free from the chute, and repel down to terra firma.

Now, logic would tell you to stay clear of the trees when you're parachuting. Sometimes the logical choice isn't best or available. However, you'll still need to make a choice, or one will be made for you. Here's a pro tip: you always have a choice. You might not like the options, but they're available to you.

When you're faced with what you think are only two choices, force your brain to search for a third. When you have only two choices, you're actually in the midst of a dilemma—your only options are this or that. When you have three options, then and only then are you making a choice!

It's easy to find two options, but you know how I feel about easy—it's the common path that leads to mediocrity. In the Spec Ops world, when you're doing a tactical mission on the ground, you avoid the common paths and roads. During a tactical training exercise in England, my training team was ambushed by instructors. Amid the chaos, my four-man team was split in half, separated. My teammate and I ran right down a highly visible common path to make it to our rally point...which happened to have been rigged by a tripwire. Luckily, that had only been a training scenario, or you wouldn't be reading this book.

It's a soft habit to walk the path you know. Soft habits get you or someone on your team killed in a combat situation. It's soft habits that will slowly kill your brand, too. What have you done today to keep your edge? **What have you done today to avoid the common path of complacency?**

Complacency leads to mediocrity. Once mediocrity is inside your restaurant, it has the same effect as inviting a bloodthirsty vampire into your home: they don't stop until they've fed on and turned everyone into what they are: Negative Energy Vamps. The best defense is to never invite them into your house. Be aware that the evil called mediocrity takes many forms. Be vigilant and remain aware of the warning signs that mediocrity has infiltrated your brand:

- Negativity
- Complacency
- Resistance to change
- Gossiping
- Cliques (mediocre vampires tend to form groups)
- Protest behavior (showing up late, not completing tasks)
- No drive to learn (happy with the status quo)
- Overcompensating confidence (acting like they know it all)

On a Spec Ops team, you don't have to like all your teammates. You do, however, need to trust that they'll have your back when the shit hits the fan. High-performance teams can only function at peak levels when trust isn't even a question. If you don't trust your team, you don't have a team—you have a group of mercenaries that will cut and run to save their asses.

Trust requires vulnerability. Don't get all freaked out. You aren't sharing the darkest secrets of your childhood or your undeclared love for someone. All that's required to be vulnerable as a team leader is to be open to what you feel that relates to the wellbeing of the team. Are you in a funk today? Okay, everyone gets in funks. Tell the team and they can up their game to protect the brand and fill in any gaps. Remember the Spec Ops Rule: **One Team, One Fight.**

Always Be Training

In Pararescue, if you're not on an operation, you're training. How your team trains is an indication of how they will perform when it counts. Those servers who only try to improve when they're working (basically, practicing on your guests over short periods) are never going to rise to high levels of performance. Have you noticed that some of the best servers have years and years of experience? Hmmm, I bet you could compress decades of experience into months with a commitment to constantly training ...maybe even going above and beyond?

Even in Pararescue, the guys were always pushing themselves beyond the standard expected level of training. Extra runs, fin swims in the pool, doing fingertip pull-ups in doorways for that little edge when climbing, shooting extra rounds at the range until they can group their shots into the lid of a Pringles can... Does a chef sharpen his knife one time, and that's it? No way. They keep their edges every day by working to keep it razor sharp!

The secret to training for high performance is this: you train to back up your team, not yourself. I was more concerned about letting my team down than I was about myself; I trained harder so that wouldn't happen. When I made the jump back into kitchens after the military, I took a job at a high-volume restaurant in Miami. I got my ass handed to me while working the sauté station on my first night. The chef had to wait for me to complete my tasks—I brought the team down. I came in extra hours, off the clock, to practice. Within a week, I was no longer the weak link on the line.

Are you more concerned about yourself or your team? Be honest. It's natural to be selfish and protect yourself. To break free from average you'll need to look at things that might not seem logical or disrupt your normal habits. You're going to have to aim for that big tree and purposely get tangled up in it. Is it going to scare you? Probably. Are you going to play it safe and stay where you are, or are you willing to go for it and jump in?

Everything you've ever wanted is on the other side of your comfort zone. How will you get there? ***Put your head down, focus, commit and move forward—one step at a time.***

Lessons from Special Ops for Restaurant Owners

My days as a Pararescueman taught me more about teamwork, adversity, peak performance, and mental toughness than I ever realized at the time. That is what makes my coaching so unique, and why I get extreme results for my clients, I am going to help you develop the mindset of an Elite Special Operations Warrior!

While the battlefield and business are quite different, they share more similarities than you would imagine. Both require you to develop yourself to reach the top. Both require discipline and grit to survive adversity. Both require that you accept NO limitations as limitations. Average people tell you to be afraid of the dark and those things that go bump in the night. The elite are the ones that bump back against dark forces that would have you play small in the world. When you adopt this level of thinking, your motto becomes: You are either on my side, by my side, or in my fucking way! *Choose wisely*.

People on your team either rise to your level or get out of your restaurant! Does that scare you to think that way? Good. We'll harness that fear and turn it into a strength you will use to become outstanding! I don't want you to shoot for greatness or even excellence...those targets are too low for the elite. It's taking your foot off the mental brakes that slow you down and slamming your foot on the accelerator...all the way to the floor!

This is what separates the excellent from the outstanding — there is no room for average where we're going. Mediocrity is a forbidden word from now on. You won't accept it from yourself any longer. You will demand more from yourself than you will ever demand from others. No more talk. It's deeds and results over words.

Here are some tools from the Special Operations world that will forge your life and your restaurant into what you desire:

Front Sight Focus

One task until it's completed. No multitasking. No changing your focus to different targets. From now on, each week, you are to have only one project that you throw all your resources into until it's done. Then and only then can you acquire a new target.

If you ever find you are overwhelmed with too many things on your plate, you need to do two things:

1. *Get a bigger plate.*
2. *Apply front sight focus on the most important project.*

Focus is the true currency for high achievers and peak performance. For some it's known as the zone. That place where time seems to stop, and you are so laser-focused that you might not even hear things going on around you. When I was a full-time chef I would experience every time I was plating a dish. No past. No future. Just the food. Just the plate. It was a Zen moment that I got to experience over and over during service.

Look at your project list and pick out one (just one) thing that has been moving along about as fast as a snail. Now, I want you to apply total front sight focus on this by taking action every single day until it's done. Do not get sidetracked. Schedule a short block of time each day to work on this! If you don't schedule time you will never make progress.

Develop a Healthy Obsession

You cannot reach the level of outstanding without becoming obsessed with reaching that level. Your goals have to become emotionally connected with your dark side. You might be saying, "My dark side? I don't have a dark side." Let me assure you that everyone has a dark side. Everyone. You might not realize it. You might ignore it. It's that voice that craves and desires. It's that push you feel about going for it. Peak Performers and those that rise to the top of this industry and stay at the top, use their dark side and do not let it use them!

Visualize Your Outcome

You must see it first. Then step into that image and make adjustments as needed. Write your goals down twice a day, read them, and picture yourself there like it's already a done deal. Just like you are watching a movie...step into it and hear what you will hear, see what you will see with your own eyes, and feel what you will feel. All the energy. All the emotions.

If you can't see it first in your head, you will never make it a reality. That is a fact. Everything that is a human-made physical object first started as an idea. If you ever started a restaurant from nothing, then you know the power of vision. Maybe you lost touch with that visionary part of yourself — time to reconnect and dream a little dream.

Pull the Trigger

Now, when you have that vision or idea in your sights, you will need to do what needs to be done and pull the fucking trigger. You must take action, and you must take action immediately! I tell all my clients this same statement so often they start finishing my sentence...*When would NOW be a good time?*

The only thing you truly have control over is the action you take at this moment. When the target is there, and you know what you need to do, then you have a duty to take action. Pull the trigger. In the Spec Ops world, hesitation can be deadly. In the restaurant world, it might not be deadly right now; however, the slow accumulation of missed targets (opportunities) start to cause damage to your confidence and brand indenting. You cannot afford for either of them to suffer if you want to thrive.

Always Be Aware of Your Restaurant

In Spec Ops, they train us to have what is known as **Total Situational Awareness**. While you are focused on your target, you still are aware of those elements in your peripheral vision. You are aware of everything going on, and you prioritize each element based on their level of threat. In your restaurant, you must know and be aware of everything going on at all times. *What is your food cost? Where are you right now for labor? Who is on the schedule, and where are they positioned? What is going on outside the restaurant that could affect business today (events, holidays, weather)?*

Now, knowing what is going on is the first part. Having a plan is the critical second part. You have to take the information and formulate a cohesive action plan with consideration for when things don't go as planned (and they often don't). *What is your contingency plan for when sales are not where you projected for the day? How are you going to drive sales to make up for the gap? How are you going to manage the extra costs that are accumulating when sales drop?* If you sit on the sidelines and wait to see what happens, you are not the leader...you are just a bystander. **Leaders take action.** They are always in action mode. There is a classic saying that rings true: *If you fail to plan, then you are planning to fail.*

Embrace the Suck

Adversity is truly a weapon if you harness its power and don't ignore or deny it. Things in your restaurant will be bad some days. They will suck. You must learn to embrace the suck and use it as an opportunity for growth. So many get bogged down in the mental quicksand when bad days happen. Life is not all sunshine and rainbows. You will have days where it rains, and you will have a few that will hit you like a category five hurricane! Embrace those days. Embrace the suck!

"Let me embrace thee, sour adversity, for wise men say it is the wisest course."

- William Shakespeare

One Team, One Fight

Your restaurant will only reach the level of outstanding when you stop fighting amongst your team. Stop this bullshit of FOH vs BOH. Stop the internal competition between locations. A divided brand is a sign of weak leadership and a toxic culture. There is an African proverb you need to write down, *"If there is no enemy within, the enemy outside can do us no harm."* In the Spec Ops world, you only survive when you harness every resource you can and employ the mindset that you are One Team, One Fight.

Violence of Action

When you first hear this, you might think that violence means hurting people; in this phrase, it means taking action with extreme focus and velocity. You make your move before others even have a chance to understand what's happening. If you have a solid plan, then you need to take violent action!

The number one advantage that independent restaurants have is that they can implement and move quickly. Large chain restaurants have a lot of corporate red tape to work through before anything is changed at the local store level.

"Let your plans be dark and impenetrable as night, and when you move, fall like a thunderbolt." - Sun Tzu, The Art of War

Slow is Smooth, Smooth is Fast

When you are training in Spec Ops, this becomes your mantra. You go through the drill slow and careful so you can break down every detail to the point where you comprehend every minute element. When you are doing drills like clearing a room and you are stacked up at the door, you don't start training full speed with live ammo. You start so slow that it almost feels like you're moving backward. Once you get that perfect, you run the drill again faster. Get that perfect, then a little faster. You do that over and over until you are going full speed with live fire.

Too many restaurants train their team at full speed right from the start. You need to slow it down so they understand the details and so you can truly access their work habits. How you do anything is how you do everything. If a new hire is careless doing basic tasks like cleaning the floor or setting a table, what chance do they have if you throw them in on the sauté station or a busy section on the floor? Not much.

Get Off the X

You can't move a mission or your restaurant forward if you are staying in the same position as you were last year. Movement or progress is always the goal. Sometimes you have to navigate around obstacles or threats; however, you are always moving towards the objective. Progress over perfection is how you should run your restaurant. Most restaurant owners have that backward and use the excuse that they need it to be perfect. While you're perfecting it, your competition is moving around you and flanking your market position.

When you are in the field and your team encounters "contact" (enemy fire), you better get off the fucking X, or you will soon find yourself in a box with a flag draped over it. In the restaurant industry staying on the X is being stuck in mediocrity. New restaurants are moving in on you, and you do nothing. You need to get off the X. *Actually, you should have gotten off the* **X** *yesterday, however, since you're just reading this now, I'll give you a break.*

Remember Howard Johnson's restaurant chain? They once had 1040 locations from coast to coast. They got sloppy and arrogant (which usually includes a little ignorance too), they thought they owned the market and refused to get off the X. There is only one location still in business as of this writing.

You Can Only Lead from The Front

Too many managers (that incorrectly call themselves leaders) think that being a leader is barking orders and being a hardass. That's being a boss. Leaders lead their team by being an example. You can't get around this. You must expect more from yourself than you do of others! That does not mean you necessarily work more. It means you are efficient, effective, and driven to lead. True leaders always want the ball in the final seconds of the game. They are driven to excel. They never rest on the accomplishments of yesterday. What you did last week or last year is nice; however you cannot win today's game with the points you scored last week! What are you doing today (right now) to move your business towards your goals? A true leader knows that success is never owned, it is rented and rent is due every single day!

Are you ready to take ownership of everything in your life? I mean, own it? The great things and those things that suck bad! Until you are ready to step up and stop placing blame on others or events that happened you will stay stuck exactly where you are and who you are. You are more than what you have for material possessions, more than the mistakes you have made in the past (I know because I have made some catastrophic mistakes.), and you have more strength and potential than you know. My duty as The Restaurant Coach™ is to assist you in unleashing that greatness, embracing the dark, and getting the fucking restaurant and life you want!

Are you in?

If, so then you have to go all in. You cannot do this with anything less than 100% commitment.

That is the price for admission to become outstanding — **all in or nothing.**

"Everyone says they're a leader until it's time to step up and do what real leaders have to do."

It's your move.

An Open Letter to Potential Clients

Excellence. It's the big word thrown around if you want to drive the team. Let me share something that might come as a shock. **Excellence sucks**. We have used that buzz word so much that it has become diluted. Do you even have a clear definition of what excellence means for your restaurant? When I ask that question of potential clients, most stumble to find the words. Many reach for generic definitions like, "too be the best," "be world-class," "Incredible food and service." When I press them for more, I get silence and more reaching for explanations (excuses). Then it becomes apparent. <u>**They're all talk, no action.**</u>

Most restaurants spend the majority of their time working or training on hard skills. Very few working on the soft skills and mental conditioning. For those that want to reach the level of becoming outstanding and not just great, that is wrong. Having solid skills, like cooking and service, are required to play the game at any level. It's those mental and soft skills that separate the elite. Discipline, leadership, culture, productivity, behavioral dynamics, core values, communication, grit...those are the traits that not only **get** you to the top; they **keep** you there.

People ask, "what is it that makes outstanding restaurants just so incredible?" It's that intangible element that they cannot seem to grasp because they have not experienced it before. I can tell you that driving a Porsche is an experience. However, if you have never driven in a high-performance car, you can't quite understand what all the fuss is about. To you, it just looks like an expensive car.

I take very few restaurant coaching clients. Why? Most can't take it. Sure, they say they want to be better and take their restaurant to the next level. They come with unrealistic expectations. It's like signing up for the gym on New Year's and expecting to be in world-class shape by the end of the month. It's not going to happen, especially if you have years of bad habits that need to be reprogrammed. That's why so many people stop going to the gym after a few weeks; they didn't realize that those bad habits were not going to go away so quietly.

Here's the thing I know. Whatever you tell me is the issue in your restaurant isn't the real issue of what is holding your business back. That issue is about five layers deeper. You've done a great job wearing the mask to the public. However, those closest to you know it. Your staff knows it. If your restaurant sales are stagnant or declining, then your guests know it too. Coaching is about building trust, so you take down the mask. Then and only then does the real work begin. I will do whatever it takes to get down to the real you. Some people don't like that. Those are the ones that never stay in coaching very long.

Only 1 in 20 restaurants that contact me about restaurant coaching make it past the initial intake call. Coaching is an equal investment for both of us. No disrespect, however, I make it clear that I work **WITH** my clients, not **FOR** my clients. It's my name on the work we do for you and your restaurant. That has to mean as much to you as to me. I am relentless in my pursuit to become better (for myself and my brands). I will work my ass off to get you where you need to be (not want to be, where you NEED to be, which is usually beyond where you think). However, I will not work harder than you for your benefit. When you become a client, you will have to play at my level, or we won't be working together very long.

When people sign up for restaurant coaching, I have **three** non-negotiable rules:

1. **Show up 100%**
2. **Do the work.**
3. **Listen.**

Show Up

Clients get private coaching calls with me at least once a week. I expect you to be on time and ready. No distractions. No driving. Be in a place that you can focus on the one thing I am focused on...**making you better**. If you can't devote at least one hour a week to your improvement, then you are wasting **your money** and **my time**. I hate wasting either.

Do the Work

You cannot stay in your comfort zone and expect new results. What you have been doing has you at the level you are now. Many times, going to the next level requires different skills, and it requires a different mindset. The things that got you here are not the things to get you to where you need to be. I will mix things up to keep you from getting comfortable. I will give you assignments and homework. Once again, you need to show me you're committed to the coaching process. If you don't invest time to complete those things, we're done. Your actions are a pure reflection of your mindset.

Listen

*Do you know the difference between **opinion** and **advice**?*

Everybody has an opinion. No disrespect to your friends, family, or people who work for you that have given you their input (opinion) on how to make your business better. If they truly knew how to get your restaurant to the next level, you wouldn't be contacting me. So, empty your cup of what you think you know. They say knowledge is power. It's not. It's just potential. Bad information is dangerous, and it's one of the primary reasons I am contacted. You took bad ideas, and now I need to get you on the right track...so we're doing things my way.

Advice is information given firsthand from someone who has been there. I see so many business coaches in the market today that have never actually owned a restaurant. Would you trust a skinny chef? No. Would you hire an overweight person to be your trainer? No, of course not. So why would you take restaurant advice from someone who's never **owned** a restaurant? Taking that even further, have they had any failures as well, learned from them, and became successful afterward? Failures are your biggest capital. That's where most learning comes from. If you're going to take advice from someone and know that it's not opinion, then make sure is from someone who's been there. Make sure they've had successes and failures. I've had both, and I've also come to terms to be able to own all of it.

What You Get That You Don't Realize

I was fortunate to be a member of the elite USAF Special Operations Teams. As a Pararescue Specialist, our job was to infiltrate behind enemy lines to recover personnel and other targets as requested by the United States of America. The school to become a Pararescueman is long and a great expense. Survival schools, Airborne School, Combat Diver School, HALO School, Mountain Rescue, Air Tactics, Close Quarter Combat, Paramedic School.

My clients might not see it; however, they are getting the same mental training that made me a Pararescueman. It's that mental game that separates the elite from the rest. Contingency thinking, front sight focus, tenacity, resourcefulness, grit, true teamwork, and leadership...those skills are developed through mental training.

There will be times you will not like what I say or tell you to do.
However, I can promise you'll love the results.

Want More?
Outstanding Mindset Booklet

Start with my booklet that will give you a step-by-step guide to having an Outstanding Day! **This booklet is available on Amazon exclusively.** Plus, I included several bonuses along with this informative booklet!

School is never out for the true professional. People who have applied the principles outlined in this booklet have experienced fantastic results. The beautiful thing about getting a taste of success is you'll want more!

Welcome to **The Outstanding Mindset Club**! Once you get the booklet, you can join the **private Facebook group — Outstanding Mindset Book —** for like-minded people such as yourself who have absorbed the content of this booklet and want to network with others who want more from themselves and their restaurants. You're the result of the people you associate with regularly. The Facebook group is your place to find peers who will push you to become your best!

Hey, it's free to become a member when you get this booklet. *When opportunity knocks, you must do your part and open the damn door.*

You need to do the work and apply the principles in this booklet to get results. Many will get this booklet, read it once, and not do one thing new to obtain the life they want. I'm betting you're not like that. I believe you'll take action and get results. Just make sure to create new habits and keep pushing yourself to change. Change is never easy. If it were, everyone would have the life and restaurant they want...**and** *we know that most don't.*

"Donald explains things honestly and candidly in 'Outstanding Mindset.' There is no sugar coating, and this is what makes Donald real. Because he tells it like it is. He isn't going to B.S. you, or tell you something nice so not to hurt your feelings. He'd rather see you succeed, prosper, and thrive than to let your own excesses be your downfall. This is what separates him from others in his industry. You'll find new techniques or familiar ones you may have forgotten about. New ideas and thoughts around the subject of time, and many more hidden gems. This is a must for anyone in the restaurant business."

-Brian Alcorn, *Owner, Paleo Brio*

The Restaurant Coach™ Podcast

This is a *free* resource. Subscribe, so you never miss an episode. It's fully loaded with interviews with leading restaurant experts, tools, and tips to get you the restaurant and life you want.

The Restaurant Coach™ (TRC) Nation

"A lot of people put pressure on themselves and think it will be way too hard for them to live out their dreams. Mentors are there to say, 'Look, it's not that tough. It's not as hard as you think. Here are some guidelines and things I have gone through to get to where I am in my career.'"

— Joe Jonas

I started **TRC Nation** as a place where sisters and brothers from the restaurant industry could gather to get solutions to real issues they face every day. Not a place to bitch and complain about how much the industry sucks, but a place where positive attitudes prevail. I truly love this industry with all my heart, and if you become a member of TRC Nation, you do too, even if you might have fallen out of love with it.

The spirit of hospitality is what drives us, and I wanted to help bring that back to the restaurant world. To do that I wanted to start a mentoring program for restaurant leaders (at all levels) to start the revolution to bring back the core values that the restaurant world once had: respect, integrity, compassion, humility, and service to others.

TRC Nation is honored to have a growing list of world-class industry experts (mentors) that are willing to donate some time each week (for an 8-week program) to help others rekindle that spark and find direction in a turbulent industry. Each mentor has been hand-picked by myself for the experience they offer and the value they bring every day to raise the standards in the restaurant industry.

How do you get a mentor? It's easy. First, apply to join **TRC Nation on Facebook** and then apply to get a mentor from the post talking about the program! Just hit **'Sign Up'** and the road to getting everything you want begins! See you inside TRC Nation!
https://www.facebook.com/groups/135011193999569/
mentorship_application/

The Restaurant Freedom RoadMAP™
Success leaves clues.

Restaurants that are incredibly successful are not lucky. Luck has very little impact on your success or failure. I know you like to think it does. It's a little more systematic than that. When you study successful restaurants for a career as I have, you do see the patterns and similarities all successful restaurants have in common.

I've broken down the exact steps that will take your restaurant from good to great to outstanding in **90 days**. The program is called **The Restaurant Freedom RoadMAP™,** and it's a step-by-step process to finally get you the restaurant you want. I've tested this program out with over 1000 restaurants, and I can say with 100% confidence that those that implement the system in the order that it is presented have produced incredible results.

Building a successful restaurant is very similar to building a house. You must have a solid foundation because, without one everything above, it will come crashing down. I designed **The Restaurant Freedom RoadMAP™** to emulate the same way you would build a home.

Start with the **foundation**. Here we put together the elements of a winning brand. You will get to understand your natural strengths. You take a strengths assessment (**ProScan® Survey**) and get some insight into how you naturally lead. We will dive into your core values with the Core ValU™ Workshop, which is critical to the long-term strength of your brand. And we will dig into why your restaurant exists in a mini-course called **KnowY™**.

After you have a solid foundation, it's time to build out the **frame** of your brand. During this phase, we will dig into creating a process map that will ensure you have the right systems in place with a program called **Restaurant Trac™**. How to attract, train, and retain top talent with my course called **The Hire Attitude™**. And then finally dive deep into maximizing your menu. I'll pull up my entire playbook on menu tricks and ways you can use psychology to increase restaurant sales in my **Menu Maximizer Workshop**™.

And then finally, it's time to put the roof on and move in! In the last module called the **function,** I will take you through the last elements needed to reach the summit of success. **The Marketing Accelerator**™ will teach you my down and dirty marketing system for restaurants that will keep your brand 'top of feed' and out in front of your competition. Next, we'll create a few strategic plans to get you consistent results using my **StratPLAN**™ and **The RestaurantMAP**™. Finally, you get my **10X Profit Plus Program**™, which until now has only been seen by my elite private coaching clients. I am going to show you how to maximize your P&L so you don't have to worry about cash flow ever again.

So, you have nothing to lose and everything to gain.

Get more info at: www.therestaurantcoach.com

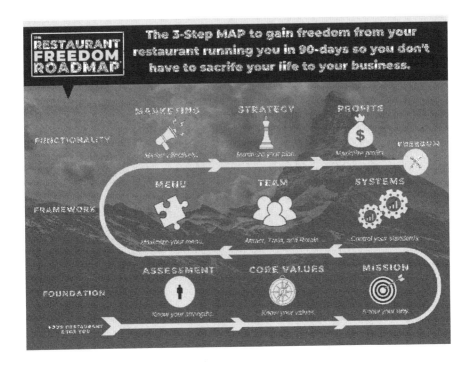

Got a Coach?
Do you have a coach?

If not, you could be limiting your restaurant's success. That's because coaches help you identify and focus on what's important, which accelerates your success.
   Great coaches:

- **create a safe environment in which people see themselves more clearly;**
- **identify gaps between where the client is and where the client needs or wants to be;**
- **asks for more intentional thought, action, and behavior changes than the client would have asked of him/herself;**
- **guide the building of the structure, accountability, and support necessary to ensure sustained commitment.**

Successful athletes understand the power of coaching. The United Kingdom Coaching Strategy describes the role of the sports coach as one that *"enables the athlete to achieve levels of performance to the degree that may not have been possible if left to his/her endeavors."*

Innovative restaurant brands understand that coaching can help their leadership team increase their performance at work. They invest in coaching for their senior leaders and high-potential employees.

Coaching also has an impact on an organization's financial performance. According to an International

Coaching Federation study, 60 percent of respondents from organizations with strong coaching cultures report their revenues to be above average compared to their peer group. When applied, coaching pays for itself.

If you are starting a restaurant and want to set yourself up for success right from the start, or if you're an existing restaurant owner who wants more, coaching is the ultimate tool.

Is coaching for everyone? **Of course not**. That's why I am willing to give you a **FREE one-hour strategy session** so you can see if coaching is right for you and your restaurant.

Follow the link to get started with a **Complimentary Strategy Session**: https://www.therestaurantcoach.com

*Restaurant coaching is <u>not</u> for everyone. Side effects include: increased profits, better staff, happier guests, stronger brand identity, reduced stress, improved relationships, and quality sleep. Talk to The Restaurant Coach™ to see if coaching is right for you.

Testimonials

"Donald really understands the hospitality landscape. As a Chef for a large food supplier, I often look to The Restaurant Coach™ to keep me on trend, find inspiration and to continue my own personal development"

-Tim Maness, Shamrock Foods, Corporate Chef Colorado

"Donald has a way to make you stop and think about how you are running your restaurant."

-Juan Pablo Vidales, Owner, Michin Kitchen

"Donald calls it as he sees it. He's not afraid to call you out on your BS but he does it with integrity, class, and gets you to reach your full potential. He won't accept anything less. He's one of a kind and has a passion for building better restaurants. Don't be one of the restaurants that suck and risk being put on the chopping block - stand out from your competitors by reading this book! You need to listen to this guy!"

-Andrew Carlson, Speaker,
Author of "Customer Service is the Bottom Line"

"Donald helped us reshape our culture through coaching. That has transformed our brand, our team, and our profits to new levels. We now spend more time working on our business and enjoying being restaurant owners."

-Todd & Candy Sheets, Owners, Sno's Seafood & Steak

"Coaching with Donald is like running your restaurant on rocket fuel!"

-Shawn Shenefield, Director of Operations, Upper Crust Pizza

"Cutting edge tools, techniques, tips and straight talk from the world's leading restaurant coach. Donald is known for unique programs and methods that create dramatic results for his clients. I asked around and found that when restaurant owners or chefs need change and want massive success they called The Restaurant Coach™. I was ready, so I contacted Donald. The coaching experience has been more rewarding than I could have ever imagined."

-Dan Palmer, Restaurant Owner

"Donald's solid, no bullshit advice is everything we needed to kick ourselves and our business into gear. He says the things no one else dares to say and holds you firmly accountable for the ways in which your business is failing, which in the end gives you the power to make things run better than you could ever have imagined, if you're willing to put in the hard graft. His advice comes from years of experience, which we only truly realized when we started putting some of the things he said into action. The results were clear from the get-go. So, take Donald's advice, put it into action and we just know you'll see the benefits immediately. This guy knows his stuff."

-David Noble, Chef/Owner, Pallett, Hafnarfjörður, Iceland

"Once we worked out our core values with Donald, we used that as a platform to base everything on, from our menu design, hiring policy, and especially our social media which really focused our message, helping us to properly engage with our customers. He helped put together an action plan to tighten our systems and get our staff more productive. Just having Donald to bounce ideas off each week gave us the confidence to take Caravelle to the level we wanted it to be."

-Zim Sutton, Caravelle, Barcelona, Spain

"Your own self-limiting beliefs are what hold you back from achieving greatness. A coach expects more from you than you expect from yourself.

Donald Burns is a coach that will tell you the hard truth when you need to hear it, give you a different perspective, and hold you accountable to push past mediocrity and excuses."

-Chef Peter Sclafani, Author "Seasons of Louisiana", co-founder of Ruffino's Restaurants

"Calling Donald just a restaurant coach is like calling Michael Jordan just a basketball player!"

-James Pecherski, Owner, Casa Taco

Become a client today to unleash your potential at www.therestaurantcoach.com

Acknowledgments

I have been fortunate to work with talented people that have helped me become the man I am today. I have always been a believer that who you associate with becomes your social and professional orbit. This list can no way include all who have made an impact on me.... *please know that you have.*

Thank you.

My OLJ Pararescue Instructors – you forged the foundation *(even if you tried to kill me)*

LD Jeffries, Clegie Chambers, Paul Pepin, Mike Buonaugurio

Culinary Mentors

Chef Jay McCarthy, Chef Terrance Brennan, Chef Wolfgang Puck, Chef Lee Hefter, Chef Matt Bencivenga (RIP), Chef Charlie Trotter (RIP), Chef Sherri Yard, Chef Francois Kwaku-Dongo, Chef Adam Lamb, Chef Chris Hill, Chef Jim Berman, Chef Craig Shelton

Badass Business Mentors & Friends

Brian Duncan, Kelley Jones, Andrew Carlson, Bruce Irving, Thax Turner, Eva Ballarin, Ken Burgin, Andrew Freeman, Doug Radkey, Bo Byrant

The Blog Wizards

Foodable TV – Paul Barron, Kerri Adams
Modern Restaurant Management – Barbara Jarvie Castiglia
Nightclub & Bar - David Klemt
Upserve – Ryan Mcsweeney, Natasha Nichols

Blood Brothers

John Trevor-Smith, Byron Kelly

My Business Coach
  Drayton Boylston

My Children
  Morgan and Alex

About db

Donald Burns is The Restaurant Coach™, named one of **The Definitive Restaurant Experts to Follow** and **One of 23 Inspiring Hospitality Experts to Follow on Twitter**.

A restaurant consultant for a $4.2-Billion-dollar company, he is the leading authority, speaker, and international coach on how restaurant owners, operators, and culinary professionals go from just **good** to becoming **outstanding.** A former **USAF Pararescueman** (PJ), restaurant owner, and Executive Chef with Wolfgang Puck, he has the unique skills to break restaurants free from average and skyrocket them to peak performance.

He works with independent restaurants that want to **build their brand, strengthen their team**, and **increase their profits** *without* sacrificing their lives to their business.

His first book: **Your Restaurant Sucks!** *Embrace the suck. Unleash your restaurant. Become outstanding.* It is an international bestseller and received the **2019 Industry Book & Author of the Year Award** by *Nightclub & Bar.*

His second book follows in the wake of his first! **Your Restaurant STILL Sucks!** *Stop playing small. Get what you want. Become a badass.*

Pick up your copy at Amazon! ***Available in Kindle and Paperback Formats.***

Made in the USA
Columbia, SC
06 October 2021